Content Analysis of Communications

Content Analysis of Communications

RICHARD W. BUDD
ROBERT K. THORP
LEWIS DONOHEW

The Macmillan Company, New York
Collier-Macmillan Limited, London

Library of Congress catalog card number: 67-16048

THE MACMILLAN COMPANY, NEW YORK
COLLIER-MACMILLAN CANADA, LTD., TORONTO, ONTARIO

PRINTED IN THE UNITED STATES OF AMERICA

To Arthur M. Barnes, Teacher and Friend

foreword

I am pleased to see the completion of this book.

Content analysis is vital to the developing sciences of human behavior, but it has had an odd history. Only recently have content analysts considered their work to be in the domain of scientific inquiry; their studies have suffered from this lack of awareness. Only recently, too, have behavioral scientists recognized that some of the things they have been doing all along are within the realm of content analysis; their work also has suffered from this lack of awareness. That is to say, content analysts are becoming more scientific and behavioral scientists are becoming more sophisticated in the great variety of techniques spawned by the content analysts — to the benefit of us all.

Somehow content analysis acquired a poor reputation among many behavioral researchers. Much of the earlier work was about as atheoretical as research can get — intended, for example, "just to describe what is there." And some of it was quite purposeful in a moralistic way — to prove, say, that "American daily newspapers do not print enough constructive news." Or foreign news. Or news about schools. Or science. Or whatever the analyst felt was an important aspect of life.

Today some of the methods of content analysis are seen as fine "unobtrusive measures"; that is, the people who produce the content that will be analyzed usually are unaware that they are being observed analytically. What they produce is often public, available for critical review by anyone. In this respect, content analytic data are different from many kinds of data communication researchers collect through questionnaires, personal interviews, and the like. In a way, they are "harder" data and they generally stand still for the researcher.

They may also be extremely important data. Have you ever stopped to think about how much of what we "know" we know only indirectly? All but the most recent history (that which has happened while we have been alive) and all but those events close enough to us for direct sensing, we have had to learn through others. Moreover, the events close to us in time and space we see only in sharply limited ways. For example,

I know a lot more about the telephone beside me than I can see, hear, or touch; I know that it can connect with any of millions of other telephones through wires and switching stations I have never seen.

These others who help us to know about things not immediately within the range of our senses may in turn have learned much of what they teach us through still others. In fact, for most of what we learn, we find ourselves on the end (no, not really the end) of a long relay and processing chain. Our historical facts have gone through many more than just primary and secondary sources. And so have many of our news facts – our current history. And our scientific facts. In these relay chains, some people exercise more freedom than others in modifying and interpreting.

The institutions, agencies, and people responsible for helping us to know our world are thus vitally important to us. How well our journalists, our teachers, and our scientists perform makes a world of difference to our well-being. Nor is this key role limited to those who supply us with factual, documentary materials. Our images of people and things not near to us in time or space sometimes derive mainly from fiction, entertainment, feature movies, and television's dramatic programs.

We need much more study of messages and the conditions under which they are produced, processed, and distributed, as well as study of what various kinds of receivers do with them. These are some of the most important social phenomena we have to investigate. I hope that we shall see much more scientific use of content analysis. With this book, the authors have done a great deal to move us in that direction.

Iowa City

Malcolm S. MacLean, Jr.
Gallup Professor of
Communication Research

preface

One of the aims of this book is to indicate some ways content analysis can be used, along with other techniques of social research, to study man's most important form of behavior—his effort to communicate with others. The book is directed mainly at those concerned with the study of the process of communication—persons in journalism, political science, speech, sociology, psychology, and broadcasting—although it should also be of use to people in areas such as history and English. It is our belief that content analysis studies should involve not only *what* was communicated, but *what kinds of people* communicated and/or in *what environment,* which may have affected the communicators in *what ways.* Many of the examples used in the book are drawn from situations involving the mass media, but it should be apparent that the content analysis techniques described here could be used to study messages produced from any communicative act.

This volume is not intended as the definitive work on content analysis nor as a summary of all the worthwhile literature in this area of communication research. Rather, we have attempted to describe and give illustrations of methods that can be used to investigate many kinds of messages. We have tried to present material that will be useful to the beginning researcher and, at the same time, to stimulate new thinking in the use of content analysis. (Thus, for example, students without training in statistics may find Chapter 9 more difficult than the other chapters.)

Because each research project is unique, the analyst must adapt, revise, or combine techniques to fit his individual problems. And because review of the literature is a necessary prerequisite to any research project, a bibliography, including representative theses and recent studies employing content analysis, has been appended. It contains more than 300 entries, which have been annotated to highlight the methodological aspects of each. Within the text, these studies are referred to by numbers in brackets to help the reader interested in investigating more fully the particular phase of content analysis being discussed.

The authors owe a considerable debt to Professor Malcolm S. MacLean, Jr., Gallup Professor of Communication Research at the University of Iowa, who has had a great deal of influence on the direction of the book. When we began work on it, he offered criticisms of content analysis as it has been practiced and suggestions for the development of the manuscript. Later, he read drafts of the manuscript, offering the kind of penetrating criticisms and ideas that every author needs—and certainly that were needed by us. This preface gives us an opportunity to publicly thank him not only for his advice on the book but also for the many other ways he has helped each of us.

We also thank Professors John B. Adams and Wayne A. Danielson of North Carolina, who generously loaned materials to us and permitted us to use quotations from their work. We are also grateful to Professors Leslie G. Moeller and James W. Markham of the University of Iowa and Bradley S. Greenberg of Michigan State for their comments and suggestions, many of which were incorporated in this work. Special thanks go to Professor Arthur M. Barnes of the University of Iowa for providing encouragement and direction of an earlier published manuscript upon which this volume is based. We also recognize the assistance and encouragement of many other colleagues and friends too numerous to mention, but without whom this project would not have been completed.

No doubt the finished work is not what any of these men would have written, nor perhaps even quite what they would have had us write. Thus, we and not our advisers must bear any criticisms.

Iowa City, Iowa
Lexington, Kentucky

R. W. B.
R. K. T.
L. D.

contents

1

content analysis and research in communication

Communicators subjected to a single stimulus – such as a news event – may produce or handle messages about the event in a number of different ways. Some may produce lengthy messages, others may produce short messages, and still others may produce no messages at all. Some may select one part of the event to report and others another part. Some may display the messages prominently; others may place them in locations where they are likely to attract little attention. These message-producing and -handling behaviors constitute a major area for communication research. There is a need not only for analysis of the messages passed along the news chains by various communicators, but also for discovery and examination of the factors in the environment to which these different kinds of behavior are related.

Let us look briefly at the world in which communications decisions are made. Every day there are thousands of events that could be selected by communicators and translated into messages. People take part in demonstrations, die in accidents, make speeches, fight with their neighbors, have a good day on the golf course, or merge their businesses. Some of these people are well known, others obscure. Any of them may be seeking to call attention to himself or his acts, or to avoid attention. Some of the events are observed, but others are not.

Communicators–energetic, lazy, experienced, inexperienced, secure, uneasy – see these events or find out about them (or do not find out about them) from other people and make decisions about which events to pass along to their audiences and in what form. These communicators may be reporters or photographers for the mass media, politicians, editors, public relations men, or others. They must decide, sometimes very quickly, whom to interview, whom to assign to cover a story, what to illustrate and from what angle, what to feature in the lead or headline, and where to put the story on a page or in a broadcast, or what to emphasize in a public address.

There is also an audience seeking information about these events—information about financial investments, personal problems, the day's developments, or entertainment. People may hear about an event on radio or television or from a neighbor and seek further details in the newspaper. They may listen to a broadcast and at the same time discuss it with a friend. They have the power to turn the dial, cancel their subscriptions, or ignore the communicators' reports. They can also tell the communicators what they like and dislike by writing letters to the editor or by visiting the producer.

CONTENT ANALYSIS—WHAT IS IT?

Many questions can be asked about these message-related behaviors, and one of the most useful tools available to investigators seeking to answer such questions is content analysis. Content analysis is a systematic technique for analyzing message content and message handling — it is a tool for observing and analyzing the overt communication behavior of selected communicators. As Kerlinger describes it,

> content analysis, while certainly a method of analysis, is more than that. It is . . . a method of observation. Instead of observing people's behavior directly, or asking them to respond to scales, or interviewing them, the investigator takes the communications that people have produced and asks questions of the communications [21, p. 544].

Content analysis allows the investigator to observe a communicator's public messages at times and places of the investigator's own choosing. The procedure also allows him to carry out his observation without fear that the attention will bias the communicator, something that would be more difficult if the analyst were trying to watch at the scene.

What the content analyst does and the contribution he can make to the study of communication can be clarified by fitting him into the diagram of the communication process (Figure 1). The diagram includes the main elements of communication: source, message, channel, and receiver. The content analyst is not part of the process, but employing his analytic tools, he taps into the process through the message to gain his primary information about the communication situation. With this information, he can give a detailed account of the communication and make limited predictions about the source and perhaps about the receiver. He does this in much the same way that researchers make predictions about behavior based on more structured attitude-measurement devices.

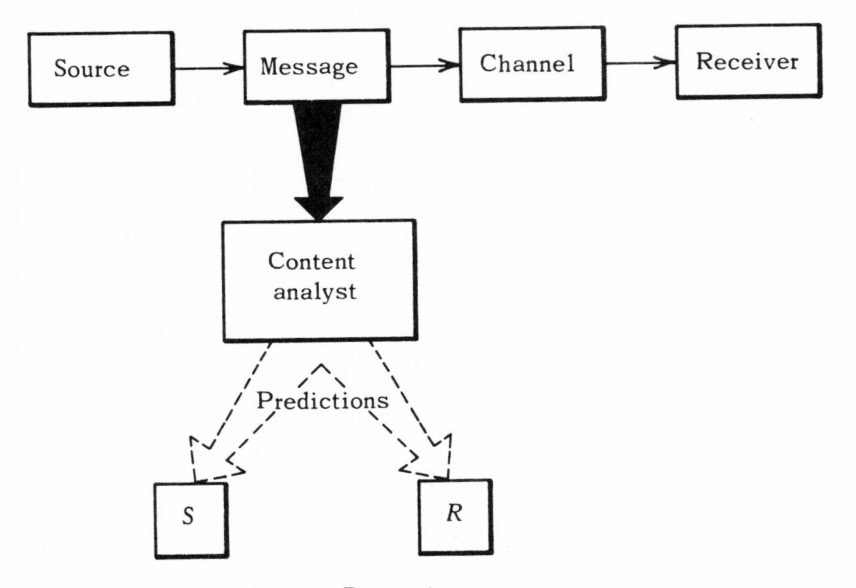

Figure 1/ Code: *S*, source; *R*, receiver.

Several years ago, Berelson defined content analysis as a research technique for the "objective, systematic, and quantitative description of the manifest content of communication" [2, p. 18]. Until recently, most users of this method appear to have concentrated only on the study of manifest content, leaving unanswered the larger question of its relation to other variables. Yet, an understanding of these relationships is a necessary prerequisite to understanding communication behavior. The ultimate goal of the investigator in the behavioral sciences is to predict behavior. To do this, he needs to find out why people do the things they do. And on his way to finding out why, he examines what things are related to what other things. The mass communications investigator may want to know, for example, why some events are reported the way they are. Why do some reporters seek out sensational details whereas others avoid them? Why are the accounts of race riots run in the lead position in some newspapers but under small headlines on inside pages of others? Why do some candidates emphasize emotional appeals whereas others lean toward rational appeals? Are these actions related to the kind of education the person has had? To what he thinks his boss thinks about the subject? To where the speeches are made? To the kinds of groups to which the communicator belongs?

Content analysis projects can help to answer these and other pertinent questions. While such projects are centered on the message produced, their object may be to find links between the message and other parts of the environment. The analyst is concerned not with the message per se but with larger questions of the process and effects of communication.

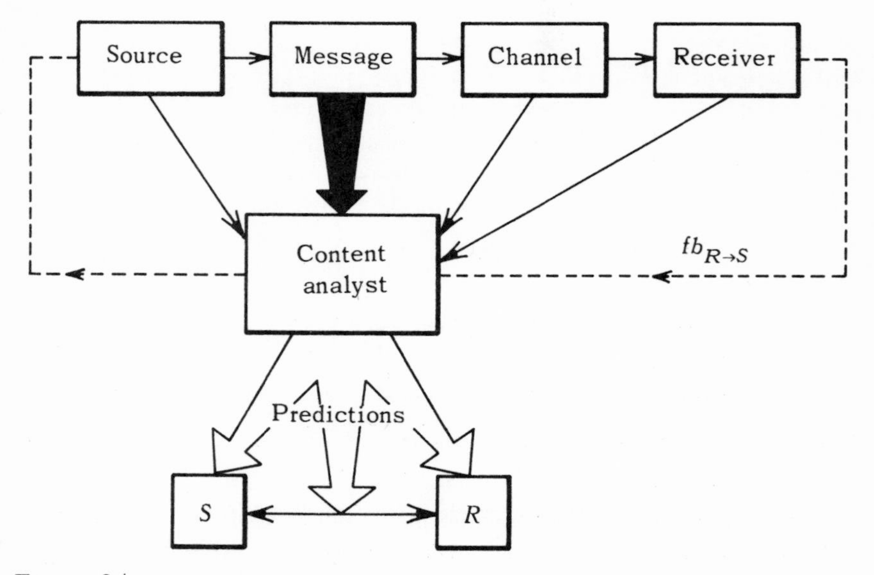

Figure 2/

If the analyst is provided with additional information (Figure 2) about the source (from studies of the communicator, for example, gatekeeper studies), the channel (from media analysis), the receiver (from audience analysis or psychological or sociological data), or feedback (by monitoring), he is able to make better predictions about the source, the receiver, and the relationship between the source and receiver. In such studies, content analysis is considered a tool to be used in combination with other techniques. Thus, where previously there was little effort to relate content variables to other variables (except in some campaign studies in which news coverage was related to political affiliation), today one may find content studies relating to such other variables as attitude, personality, or demographic characteristics.

EXTENDING THE CONCEPT

Danielson [9] observed that the trend in content analysis is toward hypothesis testing as opposed to purely descriptive research. He said that the desire to examine bias in the press is changing to a desire to examine the processes of social control in newsroom copy; and the desire to study false claims in advertising is changing to a desire to study other-directedness in advertising. He concluded that the change is toward central concepts that have more to do with abstract, theoretically oriented social and psychological concepts and less to do with relatively concrete moral issues.

While the use of content analysis in combination with other techniques permits projects of broad scope, simpler projects concentrating on content alone may still be useful—at least on some problems. While it may not contribute to our understanding of the process and effects of mass communications to know how much news about the United States is published in the South American press, or how much foreign, political, entertainment, or other news is published in a population of American newspapers, such information can often raise useful questions for this kind of research. Such inquiries merely stop a step or two sooner than the others.

Two of the outstanding figures in the study of communication have mentioned some of the needs for work in this area. Wilbur Schramm, in an essay introducing a textbook on mass communication research, issued a call for additional studies of communicators.

> It is hard to explain why journalism researchers, who of all scholars have the most right to believe they know what happens in the act of producing newspapers, magazines, and radio and television programs, have not contributed more than they have to the analysis of these communicators and what they do [32, p. 16].

Malcolm S. MacLean, Jr., has stated:

> I believe we need to study much more rigorously (the) similarities and differences among news packages and to learn much more about what factors determine them. I expect that some norms cut across every news enterprise throughout the world [269, p. 8].

MacLean added that some norms help us to recognize newspapers as such; others help us to tell one paper from another, such as the *New York Times* from the Dubuque *Telegraph-Herald;* and still others help distinguish papers of one country from those of another. There are also differences in the individuals, such as wire editors, who occupy key posts in the newspapers. These differences can be in their training, in their images of the policies and nature of the newspapers for which they work, and in their concern for what fellow editors on their own and other newspapers might think of the way they present stories. These are only a few of the many factors that might be studied in research designs employing content analysis.

Content analysis techniques may be applied to study the content of any book, magazine, newspaper, individual story or article, motion picture, news-broadcast, photograph, cartoon, comic strip, or a series or combination of any of these. They have been applied not only to printed mass media, but to such communications as private correspondence, transcripts of psychoanalytic interviews, gestures, political documents, and minutes of meetings.

STAGES OF DEVELOPMENT

Content analysis studies usually involve six stages. First, the investigator formulates the research question, theory, and hypotheses. Second, he selects a sample and defines categories. Third, he reads (or listens to or watches) and codes the content according to objective rules. Fourth, he may scale items or in some other way arrive at scores. Next, if other factors are included in the study, he compares these scores with measurements of the other variables. And finally, he interprets the findings according to appropriate concepts or theories. Discussions of these steps, which may be carried out in alternate ways, are presented in the following chapters.

2

studying communications in relation to their environment

Most researchers agree on this list of major elements in the communication process:

1/ The communicator or source
2/ The message (where content is one aspect)
3/ The channel, medium, or interpersonal networks
4/ The receiver or audience

A number of models of this process have been constructed. Such models have considerable value to the potential investigator because:

> Models allow us to isolate the parts of intricate reality that interest us and to examine the interrelationships of those parts. Models give us a way of structuring our world and of making predictions about what will happen in an "if *X*, then *Y*" sort of way [6, p. 9].
>
> Another advantage of model-making is that it brings into the open the problem of abstraction. The real world is a very complex environment indeed. An ordinary apple, for example, has a great many properties — size, shape, color, chemical composition, taste, weight, ad infinitum. In making a decision about the apple, such as whether to eat it or not, only a few of these characteristics are considered. Some degree of abstraction is necessary for decision [5, p. 17].

Some of the most useful models for students of the communication process involve the concept of gatekeepers. Lewin's gatekeeper paradigm [161] and Westley and MacLean's conceptual model for communication research [38], in which the nonpartisan role of news communicator is emphasized, have provided the base for a number of content analysis projects.

Two well-known studies exemplifying such an approach are by White [252], who concentrated on a gatekeeper of wire news, and by Gieber [109], who extended the study to sixteen wire editors within a single state receiving the same wire service. Of the gatekeeper concept, Lewin stated:

> Understanding the functioning of the gate becomes equivalent then to understanding the factors which determine the decisions of the gatekeepers .... It should be realized, however, that the forces in the gate segment of the channel will vary considerably depending on who the gatekeeper is, and upon the total situation within the channel [161, pp. 145–146].

Also commenting on this concept, Schramm noted its application to mass communications in which "at every point along the chain, someone has the right to say whether the message shall be received and retransmitted, and whether it shall be retransmitted in the same form or with changes" [33, p. 176]. Schramm noted that these gatekeepers, by saying yes or no to messages that come to them along the chain, play one of the most important roles in social communication. He added that in news chains, the news agency and telegraph editor are especially important because they are responsible for the greatest number of decisions about the passage of news along the chain.

The Westley and MacLean model (Figure 3) is discussed here as it might apply to content analysis projects involving mass media, although most of the discussion also applies to other media, such as letters or political documents. Within the kind of communications universe described in the beginning of Chapter 1, for example, messages were fashioned; we shall assume they are now available to the investigator on microfilm, newsprint, or videotape (or if the messages were transmitted by wire, perhaps on punched tape). These messages are represented on the Westley-MacLean model as X''.

Now, suppose we wish to find out whether the kinds of messages produced are related to some particular object or objects in the environments of the persons who produced them. For example, we might wish to know whether they are related to the communicator's news values learned in journalism school or on the job, to his notion of how his superiors or others might handle the events, or to other variables. These variables may be represented on the model as *X*s or *f*s, depending on their source.

One way of studying the message-producing or -handling behavior of the communicators is to compare the messages they receive with the messages they transmit. For example, if we were studying reporters' (*C*) coverage of presidential press conferences, we might get tape re-

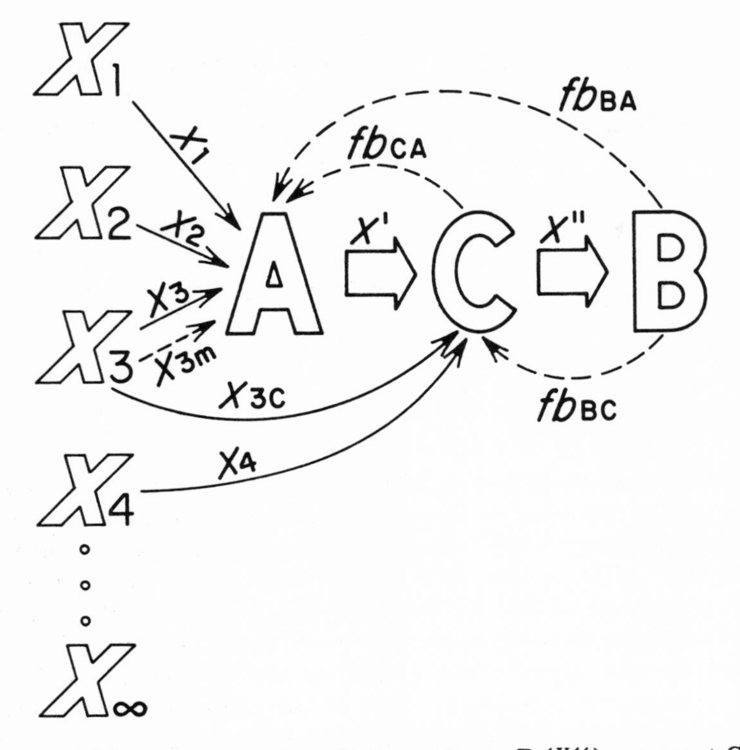

Figure 3/ The messages that C transmits to B (X'') represent C's selections from (1) the messages he receives from A (X') and (2) his selections and abstractions from the Xs in his own sensory field (X_{3C}, X_4), which may or may not be Xs in A's field. Feedback not only moves from B to A (fb_{BA}) and from B to C (fb_{BC}) but also from C to A (fb_{CA}). Clearly, in the mass communications situation, a large number of Cs receive from a very large number of As and transmit to a vastly larger number of Bs, who simultaneously receive from other Cs.

cordings of the conferences – which might contain messages (X') coming to the reporters from an *A*, the President, and from other objects in the environment, represented by X_1, X_2, X_3, and so on – and compare the messages in these tapes with the copy (X'') reporters handed in to their editors (*B*).* Or we might want to study the *C* role of wire editors, as did White and Gieber. We might want to know, for example, if some personality characteristic were related to the way they handled news about a particular kind of issue. In this case, we would measure what was offered on the wire services (X_{3C}, X_4) and

*Normally, in a mass communication situation, the B role would be assigned to the reader or viewer. In this instance, it is assigned to the editor because he is the audience for the reporter's story.

what was run (X'') in the newspapers of the editors, then compare their scores on coverage with their scores on the personality characteristic. If we wished to study a mass audience in relation to the messages, studying the output of the *C*s would tell us what was made available to our selected set of *B*s, while readership and interest measurement procedures could relate the *B*'s choices to the content and form of materials in X''. The student wishing to acquaint himself with some of the other models used in communication research will find several of them discussed in an article by Johnson and Klare [141] and a book by Alfred Smith [35].

EXAMPLES

The models discussed provide ways of structuring investigations of communication behavior so that communications are studied in relation to their environment. Many studies of this kind have been conducted without the conscious use of a model. One of the early studies in which content analysis was used as a means of observing behavior under given environmental conditions was conducted in 1950 by the Institute for Journalistic Studies at Stanford [65] during the Nixon-Douglas senatorial campaign. One of the things the investigators sought to determine was whether the editorial position of the newspapers toward the candidates was related to the news coverage they were given. Using a form of directional analysis of the news copy (in which they calculated a favored index to indicate the extent candidates were favored), the investigators found a strong relationship between editorial preference and favorable news coverage and vice versa.

A recent study involving this approach was Donohew's dissertation [288] on forces in the news channel (represented as *X*s, *A*s, and *f*s on the Westley-MacLean model), in which he used a combination of content analysis, questionnaire, scales, and demographic data to examine a communication situation. Using the gatekeeper paradigm, he sought to determine what forces were most strongly related to content and display of news about the medical-care-for-the-aged issue. The variables examined were publisher attitudes, perceived community opinions, and community conditions. In gathering data for his study, Donohew used a form of directional analysis to score gatekeeping behavior, as indicated by content and display given stories on Medicare. Publisher attitude toward Medicare and perceived public opinion were measured through a questionnaire. Community conditions—income, population aged sixty-five or over, and so on—were ascertained by gathering data from such sources as the Census Bureau and other government agencies. Ultimately, Donohew analyzed the data through use of a canonical correlation procedure carried out by a computer. Thus, the object of the study was not only to produce information about the way newspapers handled the issue, but also to provide a means of assessing the weight of various forces in the coverage and to provide an equation for predicting the way other newspapers might handle such an issue.

There are a number of ways in which study of content can be combined with other information in communication studies. Adams [41] compared data on staffing (whether or not newspapers had foreign correspondents) with scores on content in assessing the value of foreign correspondents. Stempel [223] studied editorial position, amount of news space, content direction, and makeup in examining content patterns in presidential campaign coverage. DeFleur [89] studied content of television programs for their portrayal of occupational roles, using types of occupations, background settings, interaction patterns, and relative power. He compared his findings with the proportions of these occupations in the real world. Wilensky [254] used several content analysis procedures to classify media offerings into "highbrow" and "lowbrow" categories to determine the level of media exposure and the level of culture. Some other studies using content analysis with other techniques are by Barnes and Lyness [50], Davis [85], Tannenbaum and Lynch [237], and Lyle and Wilcox [165]. These are described briefly in the annotated bibliography at the end of the book.

The variety of techniques, the numerous uses of content analysis, and the wide range of materials amenable to these techniques and uses make content analysis a tool which could be useful to almost everyone interested in communication research. Describing and defining content is basic to all communication research, although often the process is not called content analysis. A full listing of the uses of this tool is not necessary here; the reader is directed to the topics in the bibliography.

3

hypothesis formulation and systematic study

Adams has written that a content analysis project, like any other research venture, "depends upon a happy blend of researchable questions, materials to analyze, and a method" [258, p. 1]. He added that the extent of satisfaction in the finished product depends on how closely all three elements match ideal standards.

Research is often characterized as a search for solutions to a problem. In many instances the problem may be presented most usefully by hypotheses that focus on crucial questions suggested by the problem. As Adams noted, the potential investigator must have a problem that can be stated in a way that lends itself to a systematic search for the answer. For example, he might have some notions about the behavior of mass communicators under certain conditions. These notions would be stated in the form of hypotheses. A hypothesis, according to Kerlinger [21], is a conjectural statement – a tentative proposition – about the relation between two or more observed phenomena or variables. It states in a way that can be tested how the variables are related. In stating a hypothesis, the investigator will probably say: "If these conditions are present, the communicator will behave in that way." An actual project will supply an example.

Adams wanted to explore the broad question: Of what value is it to a newspaper's readers for the paper to have its own correspondents abroad? One of his most important tasks was to restate this question in a way that could be systematically investigated. His notions about the differences in the content between newspapers with correspondents and those without correspondents were presented as a set of hypotheses. The first two of them and their rationale are presented here.

> First of all, it would seem that "better" foreign news coverage would include "more" foreign news. In this case it was hypothesized that:
>
> 1/ The average length of foreign news stories will be significantly greater in newspapers with staff abroad than in newspapers without such representation.
>
> While it is granted that counting column inches tells nothing about the quality of what is in the space, part of "better" coverage would seem to be found in longer stories, presumably providing more details or deeper analysis.
>
> A second indication of a newspaper's attention to foreign news is the use of the front page for such stories. Since all newspapers have about the same front page space, gross differences would not be expected, but it was hypothesized that:
>
> 2/ Proportionately more foreign news stories will appear (or begin) on Page One in newspapers with staff abroad than in newspapers without foreign correspondents [41, p. 301].

It should be noted that the hypotheses fit the "if this, then that" model suggested. In the study quoted here, Adams investigated a total of six hypotheses. The hypotheses were tested by comparing the foreign news content of two groups of newspapers – one group with an overseas staff, the other without one. As indicated in his hypotheses, Adams expected that certain significant differences in foreign news coverage would indicate that readers of the newspapers with an overseas staff have available better foreign news coverage than readers of the papers without their own correspondents. A chi-square test was used to determine the probability that differences between the two groups could have occurred merely by chance.

BACKGROUND

To the person well read in communication concepts and familiar with studies carried out in this area, research problems may be found almost anywhere. It has been said that a good photographer may see (and shoot) outstanding pictures while standing beside other photographers who produce routine pictures. Similarly, the person familiar with the theoretical background of communication and the work that has contributed to its development may see and produce good studies from what might appear to be nonrewarding situations to the less well versed.

The investigator may develop some studies in an effort to shed light on questions raised in previous work about which he has read, such as the problem of studying effects of communications over long periods of time. Or he may develop others in an effort to show the effects on communications situations in work going on in other areas of the social sciences, the physical sciences, or some other area. He also may draw upon his own experience for research ideas. For example, he may be a former newspaper reporter who remembers the efforts of clubs to get items printed and their competition to have the best scrapbooks of clippings. This may lead to a study of face-to-face demands made on mass communicators by groups in his community. He might do something as simple as having someone (other than the newsmen contacted by the groups) record, for a selected time period, the number of times representatives of given clubs enter or telephone the newsrooms of the papers in his sample. He then could correlate this with space-display measures of news about the clubs. Or he may attempt more sophisticated measurement of these pressures for publicity.

After the investigator is familiar with the background and has decided upon a project, he may do quite a bit of exploratory reading if the study will involve content analysis. Kerlinger notes that in reading minutes of board meetings, for example, an investigator may notice that certain boards tend to reach unanimous decisions, while others rarely show unanimity. He may also notice that one kind of board tends to be better educated than another kind. It is from such observations that good hypotheses are born.

Although good hypotheses contribute to precision, the investigator may wish to conduct an exploratory study in which he wants to observe only what would happen if he introduced a selected stimulus under certain conditions or went about his study in a particular way. MacLean [27] has observed that a good deal of trial-and-error effort also may be fruitful because there are many communications problems about which there is little knowledge.

THE SYSTEMATIC APPROACH

The projects mentioned above are examples of systematic approaches to the study of communications behavior using content analysis. A more precise description of this approach is offered by Kerlinger.

> Scientific research is systematic, controlled, empirical, and critical investigation of hypothetical propositions about the presumed relations among natural phenomena [21, p. 13].

Most simply, it is research that is planned in regard to theory, then executed according to that plan. The researcher writes a clear statement of the research questions, considers ways to obtain the necessary data, and writes a step-by-step description of the procedures, including what analyses will be made. Systematic research generally includes hypotheses, such as those described, that can be tested through analysis of the data collected.

An important requirement of systematic research is that it be carried out in such a way that its results can be verified by other investigators who follow the same steps as the original researcher; that is, both the original investigator and those who follow him should get essentially the same results. Thus, the person carrying out a project should include in his design some way of checking the reliability of his results. In the Adams study, for example, coders had to make some judgments in classifying materials. To check consistency, Adams had pairs of coders classify the same material, unaware that other coders had worked on it. He then ran intercoder reliability checks, which showed correlations of .89 to .96 on the materials coded. These procedures are discussed in greater detail in Chapter 8.

The scientific researcher does not start out to prove something; he merely sets out to investigate – and he must be careful to design his own prejudices out of the study. Reliability checks are applied, in part, as a means of gaining objectivity. Systematic methods of content analysis, when properly used, can eliminate much of the possible bias of the investigator. This calls for a sound design and rigorous adherence to the procedures set forth. Moreover, when the counting (or coding) has been completed, the results must be capable of mathematical manipulation – correlations, averages, tests of differences, and so on – which are discussed in Chapter 9.

Counting or measurement of some sort obviously is the basis for any quantitative study. Along with measurement there usually is a classification of items among various categories. The researcher may arrange the data to show, for example, trends or similarities or differences among categories, depending on the aims of his research. The trend in content analysis is toward more scientific studies, in keeping with trends in other forms of communication research – toward more precision, reliability, and useful information.

Although certain requirements are common to all systematic research projects, the choice of investigative techniques must be highly flexible because there are many different kinds of problems that can be studied. In discussing these requirements in the following chapters, the authors offer a number of alternative procedures. The choice of those used depends on the questions to be answered in a particular project.

4

sampling

For many content studies, the immense task of analyzing various aspects of the content in all the space of all issues of all publications for the entire time period would inhibit the investigator from the outset. Fortunately, there is ample evidence that properly selected samples can give adequate descriptions of very large quantities of content. Furthermore, such samples allow the investigator to estimate statistically how much his descriptions might be in error. Sampling theory is one of the most advanced fields of the behavioral sciences. This chapter is concerned with applications of sampling principles to content analysis.

In studies involving sampling, we make observations of a limited number (sample) of individuals, objects, or events so that we can make inferences about the larger number (universe or population) from which we have drawn the sample. For example, we might wish to describe United States daily newspaper coverage of political-diplomatic-governmental events during the past year. Obviously, if we chose to analyze all such items in all issues of the 1,760 United States daily newspapers for last year, the study might have only historical interest by the time we finished it. But, by examining a tenth, for example, of such space in twelve issues of each of fifty daily newspapers, we could finish the job quickly and get reasonably accurate estimates (percentages, averages, correlations) for the whole population of United States daily newspapers. That is, we could if we followed correct sampling procedures.

RANDOMNESS

One of the most important principles in sampling theory and practice is the random draw or random assignment. In this sense, random does not mean haphazard – nor does it mean scooping up those newspapers you can get most conveniently. Randomness refers to chance occurrence such as the heads-or-tails outcome of a well-spun, unbiased coin; or the count of well-shaken, well-thrown, unbiased dice; or the distribution of cards in a hand dealt from a well-shuffled, unbiased deck of cards. Nothing but chance, pure chance, must determine the drawing of units of the universe into the sample. Though randomness at first seems like meaninglessness, it does not mean that you cannot design samples to achieve meaningful purposes.

How can you get a random draw in practice? There are various ways. One of the easiest and best is to use a table of random numbers. An excerpt from such a table has been reproduced below. For drawing a simple random sample, all you need do is number all the sampling units in the population, properly enter a table of random numbers, and identify the units whose numbers appear in the table until you have reached the size of the sample you wish.

Table 1/ Table of Random Numbers

	00–04	*05–09*	*10–14*	*15–19*	*20–24*	*25–29*	*30–34*	. . .
00	96758	87010	13861	51273	18404	95321	01732	. . .
01	31018	41871	68605	41271	03560	20347	20773	. . .
02	53838	60727	16048	39188	38763	18736	18156	. . .
03	95191	25824	41213	21531	38962	05618	73997	. . .
04	38176	20646	06312	51212	08396	04233	38893	. . .
05	98018	36803	18448	06826	47820	17475	53200	. . .
06	91388	47464	41669	50097	35641	72829	57030	. . .
07	69294	77264	15770	32013	35810	07075	60830	. . .
.	.	.	.	.	.	.	.	. . .
.	.	.	.	.	.	.	.	. . .
.	.	.	.	.	.	.	.	. . .

For example, assume you have three months' issues of newspapers from which you want a sample of fourteen. With the newspapers arranged sequentially by date, number each issue 1 through 91. Now you are ready to enter the table of random numbers. Normally, such tables will be arranged like Table 1. The two-digit numbers down the left side are row numbers; the numbers above each column of five-number groups are column numbers. To enter the table, you need a random entry point for rows and another random entry point for columns. One way to get these numbers might be to ask a friend for his birth date. Assume the date is

February 18, or abbreviated, 2-18. You may use the 2 as the entry point for rows and the 18 as the entry point for columns. Using Table 1, the random number arrived at is 8. Since you need two numbers (01–91) in this case, you can arbitrarily choose to use columns 18 and 19 from which to draw numbers. This means the first random number is 88 – the issue with the corresponding number becomes part of the sample. Because the numbers in the table are random (without pattern or bias), you may now proceed either vertically or horizontally. If you continue downward, the next number is 31, followed by 12, 26, 97, and so on. Continue down the column until fourteen issues have been drawn.

Now, what happens if you should reach the end of columns 18 and 19 before you have the required number of sampling units? Simply move to the top of the table and use columns 20–21. If a number turns up twice, just ignore it the second time. Likewise, if no such number exists in the universe (for example, 97 in the sample above), ignore it and continue.

DEFINING THE POPULATION

Generally, if you make a clear statement of the purpose of your study, it will include a clear operational definition of your population. Until you have defined your universe in a workable manner and have decided what to use as a sampling unit, you are not ready to sample. Here are some examples of clear definitions:

1/ All nonadvertising pictorial (nonverbal) content in *Life* magazine (published by Time-Life, Inc.), United States edition, since its inception in 1936 to the last issue of 1965

2/ All news items concerning the United States published in eight selected foreign daily newspapers commencing February 20, 1966, and ending May 13, 1966, excluding those items in issues published on Sundays

3/ All front pages of United States evening daily newspapers with a circulation of at least 10,000, but less than 50,000, copies, excluding Saturday and Sunday issues, during the months of April and May, 1965

SAMPLING UNITS

The findings of most content analysis studies will probably be expressed in terms of the relative frequency of occurrence of some unit such as the column inch, item, paragraph, theme, or key word. The selection of one of these units over another for expressing the findings depends on the purpose of the study and the kind of content being analyzed.

Many research questions can be answered with the gross information provided by the mere measurement of space or counting of items. In such cases, sampling whole articles or using whole articles as sampling units will suffice. If the sampling unit is to be smaller, such as a paragraph or theme, a two- or three-stage sampling procedure may be necessary. A sampling unit called the basic space unit, which incorporates a number of features, has been developed and is discussed at length later in this chapter. Whatever sampling unit is chosen, the sampling procedure is the same. Sampling units must be selected from a universe of units, and every unit in the universe must have an equal opportunity to be included in the sample.

In 1952, Berelson [2] pointed out a distinction between kinds of units that still has meaning. He said that the recording unit (that unit being counted and processed) may be included in a larger unit called the context unit. The smaller unit is the unit being classified, but in order to classify it properly, the larger context unit is required to give meaning to the smaller. Such would be the case with thematic or assertion analyses.

SAMPLE SIZE

How big should your sample be? The best answer to that is, "It depends." How precise must your percentages and means be, as estimates for those for the universe? How similar are your sampling units in respect to the characteristics you are analyzing? How much time and money do you wish to invest in the study? How much are you going to break the sample down into smaller subsamples for analysis? Can you increase your precision substantially by stratification? To what extent will clustering effects reduce the precision of your sample? For answers to these questions and others that will be raised by your particular study, you should refer to one or more of the several good statistics books listed in the bibliography.

Regardless of the type of sampling procedure the analyst chooses, the general requirements of randomization and probability sampling must be observed. In addition, most content studies require multistage sampling procedures, i.e., several different sampling procedures have to be used before the final sample of content to be analyzed is obtained. In a study of daily newspapers of a certain size, for example, it would be necessary first to sample titles, then to sample issues of the selected titles, then to sample articles, and then perhaps—depending on the study—to sample the content of the articles.

Viewing the content analysis sampling problem from this point of view, varying sample sizes might very well be needed for varying aspects of the same study. The question of sample size has received considerable attention from a number of researchers involved in content studies. For most purposes in content analysis, according to Berelson [2], "A small, carefully chosen sample of the relevant content will produce just as valid results as the analysis of a great deal more—and with the expenditure of much less time and effort." However, Lasswell, Lerner, and Pool [24] cite the relationship between design and sample size: "Unless one is interested in the most common symbol or group of symbols, a rather extensive sample size is necessary. The reading necessary to cover such an extensive sample, however, places strict limits on how extensive the analysis can be." In other words, if the measuring device employed is capable of producing only coarse measurements meant solely to answer very general questions, a relatively small sample will probably serve quite well. However, if one is attempting to determine the presence of or relationship among a relatively large number of symbols or categories, the size of the sample will have to be large, since some of the symbols may appear less frequently or not at all in a very small sample.

There has been considerable research into the problem of determining adequate sample size for the study of communication content. Stempel attacked the problem of determining adequate sample size for the classification of subject matter published in daily newspapers.

> To investigate this question we examined a single subject-matter category for a single newspaper for an entire year, thus getting a universe parameter to compare samples to.
>
> We drew ten samples each of sizes six, twelve, eighteen, twenty-four and forty-eight and compared the averages to the average for the entire year. We also compared the sets of samples to each other.
>
> Our results indicate that for a single category all five of the sample sizes do an adequate job and that increasing the sample sizes beyond twelve does not produce marked differences in the results [225, p. 333].

Since these findings were published, a number of studies have been conducted employing relatively small samples. Hachten [117], for example, studying Sunday newspapers published from 1939 through 1959, employed Stempel's reasoning. Hachten drew only 3 issues to represent each year in the study, reasoning that if 12 issues are an adequate sample of a universe of 312 (the number of issues published by a daily paper during one year on a 6-issue-per-week basis), 3 issues should be an adequate sample for a Sunday paper with 52 annual editions. While this study exemplifies the use of a small sample, we should like to point out that there are dangers in a sample that is too small. Small samples can contribute to large sampling errors. To the beginning researcher, Kerlinger says:

> Use as large samples as possible. Large numbers are not advocated because large numbers are good in and of themselves. They are advocated in order to give the principle of randomization, or simply randomness, a chance to "work," . . . [21, p. 61].

Markham [169], in his study of foreign news in the United States and South American press, employed a sample of thirty issues of each publication studied to represent a three-month period. Hart [121], studying the use of foreign news in Ohio metropolitan dailies, used eighteen issues to represent a three-month period. In conducting a content analysis of radio and television newscasts, Ecker [289] employed newscasts given on ten separate days to represent a universe of one month. Clark [287], studying the use of wire copy by Iowa evening newspapers, used ten days to study wire copy over a 2½-month period. Both samples employed rotating sampling procedures (a form of stratification) to ensure an equitable distribution of days. It should be noted, however, that, with the exception of the Stempel study, none of these investigations compared its findings for the sample with measurements taken for the entire time period of the study. A 1959 study by Jones and Carter [142] in a sense replicates the Stempel test of representativeness. Jones and Carter tested a sample of six issues of a daily newspaper and found that the estimates derived from this sample were close to the averages found when the entire universe (a one-month period) was analyzed.

There is a limit to how small a sample can be and still provide valid results. The studies cited above were discussed to indicate how small samples can be and have been used. If the content to be analyzed is homogeneous, it is possible that a small sample can be very precise. In other circumstances, a larger sample usually is necessary to allow a deeper analysis of content.

Random-sampling error is not the only source of error in sampling procedures. Other sources of errors can be controlled to a great extent, and their effect upon the validity of the sample is quite dependent on the methods used in drawing the sample. These methods will be discussed in conjunction with three basic problems common to most content analyses in which sampling procedures are used.

TYPES OF SAMPLING

Before discussing the common problems of sampling content, perhaps a brief description of the basic types of sampling would be helpful. There is no best sampling plan that can or should be used in all circumstances. Much depends on the specific problem at hand, the materials with which the analyst is working, and the characteristics of the content to be studied. The best sampling plan is that which holds the standard error as small as is practical.

The basic form of sampling is called the simple random method, in which every unit in the population has an equal and known probability of being selected because each is drawn from the population independently of the others. The theory holds that in such sampling, characteristics of the population will be represented in proper proportion in the sample. Other sampling techniques are modifications of this procedure, preserving the concepts of randomization and equal probability.

STRATIFICATION

Stratified random sampling refers to the classification of the population by relevant criteria (circulation size, time of publication, geographic location, political inclination, etc.) into *strata;* then a random sample is drawn from each cell. No single unit should appear in more than one stratum; at the same time, no unit must be omitted from the strata. Once the sample is drawn, the units selected are put together to give an estimate of the population.

INTERVAL

Interval (or systematic) sampling refers to the selection of sample units at specific intervals. Suppose, for example, you wanted to select a sample of 30 issues of a seven-day daily newspaper. Your universe would be 365 consecutive publication dates. To find the limits of the starting point, divide 365 by 30. The result is 12.2, which means that every member of the population has approximately a one-twelfth chance of being selected. Using a table of random numbers, you would choose a number between 1 and 12, and then select every twelfth date until the sample was complete. If the random number were 8, you would select 8, 20, 32, 44, and so on, until you had thirty issue dates. Obviously, there are dangers in this system of sampling. For example, if your predetermined sample size happened to be fifty, your interval would be about seven and you would end up with a sample of fifty issues all from the same day of the week. Because of the trends and cycles that appear to be present in the flow of news, interval sampling is seldom used in studies of content.

CLUSTER SAMPLING

When clusters or groups of units are used as the sampling unit, they are usually made up of existing components (a city block, for example) and are not constructed by the researcher purely for obtaining a cluster sample. In the sense that a complete issue of a newspaper represents a cluster of articles, cluster sampling is used quite often in content analysis. However, it is probably not usually considered in these terms.

MULTISTAGE SAMPLING

While not a separate sampling procedure in itself, multistage sampling has central importance in content analysis. The term refers to the selection of samples sequentially, using the same procedure or a combination of procedures. Titles may be selected by simple random or some form of stratified random sample; issues, by clusters of weeks or (again by stratified random sample) of days; and articles in the issues, by some pure random method. This procedure will become clearer as we discuss some of the particular problems of sampling content.

SAMPLING PROBLEMS

Berelson indicates that there are at least three distinct decisions to be made concerning sampling in content analysis. They involve three distinct universes from which samples must be drawn, and as noted, the sampling procedures involved can differ with each universe.

> First there is the problem of sampling *titles* (i.e., specific newspapers or radio stations or magazines); then there is the problem of sampling the *issues* or *dates* of the titles; and finally, there is the problem of sampling the relevant *content* within the specific issues and titles [2, pp. 176–177].

TITLES

How one goes about sampling titles depends, of course, on the nature and purpose of the study. Often, this phase of the sampling problem can be accounted for in the statement of the problem. Berelson suggests a number of criteria – each of which could serve as the basis for stratification – to use for the selection of titles: (1) geographic areas; (2) types or presumed audience; (3) editorial direction (conservative, liberal, political affiliation); (4) size or importance (metropolitan, small city, weekly); (5) ownership and control; and (6) time of issue (e.g., morning or evening). A survey of the literature, primarily those studies listed in the bibliography, indicates that titles were rarely selected by random-sampling methods; in most cases, they were selected purposively.

Arbitrary selection of titles should normally be avoided. Even if the number of titles in the universe is small, random sampling seems to offer the best methods of selection. In sampling titles, the researcher usually finds that stratification of the population is advisable. If one were interested, for example, in studying the general content of all dailies in the United States, such a study could be accomplished through the use of a random sample. With the help of a master source (such as *Editor and Publisher Yearbook* or the *N. W. Ayer and Sons Directory of Newspapers and Periodicals*), all dailies in the country could be stratified according to one, all, or any combination of the criteria outlined by Berelson. Once the universe is stratified, the analyst may proceed to draw a random sample from each stratum. The sample could then be checked against the universe to see how representative it is. McCaffrey [297] used this technique to draw a sample of Iowa weeklies. One could, of course, follow the same procedures in sampling radio or television stations (e.g., on the basis of power or network affiliation) or magazines (usually on the basis of audience or frequency of publication).

The size of the universe (perhaps as small as twenty or twenty-five titles) should not lead the researcher into believing he might be able to construct a better sample than chance can. If he is concerned about matters of dual ownership, location, or size, he can make allowances for these factors by proper stratification of the universe. The final selection of titles for study should still be by random-sampling methods.

A number of the content analysts whose studies are listed in the bibliography selected their sample publications by a method sometimes referred to as *purposive sampling*. This procedure appears to be a type of best-guess selection based on the analyst's own knowledge of the publication; the analyst personally decides which titles would best represent the area in which he is working. It should be made immediately clear that this technique, while widely used, is not a method of probability sampling; therefore great caution must be exercised in generalizing from the findings of studies that use this sampling method to all other units comprising the population from which the samples are selected.

In most of the cases in which purposive sampling was employed, the criteria used by the researchers for the selection of various publications could have served as bases for stratification and the actual selection process could have been carried out randomly. For example, Merrill [178] selected ten Mexican dailies on the basis of geographic location, ownership, and size. Studying trends in Sunday newspapers, Hachten [117] used, in addition to geographic location and size, papers considered "important in their own right" and those that represented the usual Sunday formula in both content and format. While admittedly the latter two criteria are ambiguous, they could be operationalized for sampling purposes.

Comparative studies often involve special problems, but procedures are available for drawing matched samples randomly. In comparative studies, the analyst is usually trying to match titles having similar characteristics, such as circulation, size of city served, or wire service availability, in addition to finding overall characteristics of representativeness. Conrad [73] faced this problem in the study of social images in the East German and West German press. Nixon and Jones [187] matched competitive papers in a study of general news content. Budd [63] also matched papers on the basis of relative size of cities and geographic location. In each of the studies cited, random-sampling techniques were not used when they probably could have been, and all the studies suffered somewhat in their power to generalize. This is not to say that credible jobs of content analysis cannot be done employing this sampling technique, but such studies are quite definitely limited to specific problems. For example, Karius [296] conducted a study of the Milwaukee newspapers before and after merger. While his findings might be very useful in describing the specific situation in Milwaukee, he would not be at liberty to draw inferences about mergers in general.

If the researcher finds himself in a position to employ the purposive sample, he should be familiar with all the elements of his study, for example, content, nature of the publication, and nature of the audience.

ISSUES

Another sampling problem facing the researcher is that of determining which issues or dates of the titles are to be selected for study. This particular problem, however, can often be solved by standard random-sampling methods. Again, before drawing a sample of issues, the universe from which the sample is to be drawn must be adequately described and its limits specifically defined. This generally means specifying the time period under study—a period that should be clearly stated when defining the universe. Many studies span a period of only a few days, in which case a census might be in order; other investigations cover periods ranging from a few weeks to several years and are therefore adaptable to some form of random sampling.

In the case of daily newspapers or daily radio broadcasts, a common sampling unit is the calendar date. One approach to sampling dates, which has been tested for validity is the constructed time period. This method of sampling was devised by Carter and Jones [142] in a study devoted to procedures for determining the size of a newspaper's news hole. They created an artificial week consisting of six days, Monday through Saturday, by drawing calendar dates randomly from a three-week period (the defined universe). To ensure an equitable distribution over the three-week period, the authors stipulated that not more than two days could be drawn from any one calendar week. In other words, the universe was stratified by both days and weeks to ensure an equal distribution of both. The following example shows what a constructed week drawn from a three-week period might look like:

M	T	W	T	F	S
1	*X*	3	4	*X*	6
X	9	10	11	12	*X*
15	16	*X*	*X*	19	20

In this example, the *X*s indicate the days selected. Notice that the days are not necessarily selected consecutively. For example, the Monday in the constructed week actually follows the Tuesday and Friday included in the sample.

This procedure was adapted and expanded by Budd [63] in drawing a constructed month from a three-month period. Markham [169] drew a sample of thirty calendar dates from a three-month period but made no attempt to equalize the number of Mondays, Tuesdays, Wednesdays and so on; he employed a table of random numbers to make his selections. Clark [287], studying wire-copy usage by Iowa dailies, created a systematic week by a rotating sampling procedure. The sample period began on Monday of the first week, the second sample day was Tuesday of the second week, then Wednesday of the following week, and so on, until two five-day weeks had been completed. While Clark's procedure is acceptable, the beginning point in such a method should be determined randomly to allow every member of the population an equal chance of selection. Ecker [289], studying radio and television newscasts, accomplished essentially the same thing by sampling only odd calendar dates over a one-month period. Again, however, the selection of odd or even days should be made randomly.

There is good reason for attempting to stratify the sample for days of the week and weeks of the entire time period studied. It is well known that the news volume in any medium varies from day to day. For example, on Mondays there is usually not a great deal of news from government agencies on any level because most government offices are closed on Sunday. On the other hand, one is unable to predict the societal eruptions that make news under modern definitions. Therefore, when studying a period such as one, two, or three months, one should attempt to compensate by seeking a distribution that will, in the long run, represent the time period equitably. There is available to the researcher a simple statistical technique to test the hypothesis that a sample drawn in this manner is random. The test, commonly known as the runs test is based on the order or sequence in which the individual scores or observations are drawn. In this particular case, these observations would be calendar dates. This test is outlined in detail in Siegel [34].

In working with daily newspapers, the analyst might be faced with an additional problem of selecting issues – which edition of each paper to use. Yu [309], in his analysis of news concerning China in the four large Chicago dailies, solved this problem by using the edition of the paper that reached the greatest number of people. Other criteria such as the latest edition published each day or time of publication also serve, and the particular problem to be solved might suggest the best solution. The researcher should be aware that such a problem exists and should use the same edition throughout the analysis.

Earlier in this chapter we mentioned types of fluctuations that might occur through trends and cycles. The presence of trends and cycles is perhaps another forceful influence for considering stratification in the selection of issues. Lasswell, Leites, and their associates list a number of nonrandom fluctuations to be taken into consideration, including cycles and trends.

> The frequent existence of primary trends in material, such as frequencies of different categories ... may be taken for granted. However, there are trend fluctuations of different types. A trend may be linear, representing a constant rate of increase or decrease of a certain percentage. But it also may be curvilinear, the rate of increase or decrease not being constant during the time interval; for instance, the increase may not continue for a whole month, or may be followed by a decrease after the percentage reaches a maximum.
>
> A sample consisting of data on several separate nonconsecutive days should largely eliminate the disturbing effects of the different kinds of trends. Consecutive days tend to over-represent a particular part of a trend [23, pp. 129–132].

Cyclical trends are, in effect, the same as primary trends except that they operate over longer periods of time. For example, Sunday papers or newscasts are quite generally different from newscasts offered on weekdays. Certain types of events such as football games take place only on weekends. To use another example from the realm of sports, the periods between the ending of one sport's season and the beginning of another usually are attended by a reduction in sports news. Governmental news is somewhat reduced during the periods in which Congress or state legislatures are not in session. Political news reaches a disproportionate high during September, October, and early November.

The problem of noting trends and avoiding atypical periods of content is also present in studies covering long periods of time. Singel [302], in a study of the rise of *Mademoiselle* magazine, sampled the years 1940 (prewar), 1946 (postwar), 1951 (as an intermediate year), and 1957 (as the current year). Singel felt that in the overall development of the magazine, the war years would have provided a picture that was not typical. In a study of the image of the scientist in science-fiction stories, Hirsch [135] provided a sampling procedure with some merit. He divided the years from 1926 through 1950 into six subperiods, roughly corresponding to internal historic events (e.g., 1926 to 1929, prosperity). He then drew a random sample of fifty stories from each of the six strata. Baker [280] applied a similar rationale in a study of the rise of do-it-yourself themes in American magazines since 1939. Hachten [117], studying trends in United States Sunday newspapers from 1939 to 1959, selected newspapers at five-year intervals. From each year he selected February, June and October as normal periods of newspaper publication; most schools were in session and national holidays did not affect publication. Note that each of these sampling methods differs from the others in light of the particular problem under study.

SPACE UNITS

After selecting the titles and issues or dates, the analyst may still find the content to be studied too voluminous for analysis. Nevertheless the objective of the project might be met by studying only a sample of the content. Although a great deal of research has contributed many methods of sampling issues and titles, little attention has been directed to sampling content. Most of the studies noted in the bibliography simply avoided the problem of sampling content by coding all the relevant material published. This procedure has given content analysis the reputation of being a tedious, laborious, and almost depressing form of research. Only recently was the problem of sampling content attacked systematically. Danielson and Mullen [83], noting that too often the solution to avoiding the tedious job of coding great volumes of content is to reduce the size of the title or issue sample (which may be detrimental to the study), suggest a method of sampling content called the *basic space unit* (BSU). In their search for such a unit, Danielson and Mullen set out four criteria the unit should meet.

1/ The unit had to be large enough to yield meaning.
2/ It had to be small enough not to contain too many meanings.
3/ It had to be easily identifiable.
4/ The total number of units in the issues to be sampled had to be easily ascertainable for sampling purposes [83, p. 108].

Past attempts at sampling content employed such natural units as the article, paragraph, column inch. Danielson and Mullen rejected the article as being too large, carrying too much meaning; the column inch was rejected because it was not easily identifiable. Substituting for these natural units, the two researchers developed the basic space unit (BSU), a variable space measure which they defined as "an area one column wide and one-twentieth of a column deep." As Danielson and Mullen note, the measure approaches the column inch but has the advantage of varying in proportion to variations in page length from paper to paper. In a standard eight-column newspaper, even with variations in size, there are 160 BSUs per page. In any study of length, this unit makes possible quite a large universe from which to sample.

When the universe has been defined, the analyst may proceed to employ the standard random-sampling techniques that suit the problem. A computer program for drawing such samples has been devised by Danielson and Mullen. Input of the program contains the name of the newspaper, number of issues, number of pages in each issue, and size of the sample of BSUs desired. Output of the program consists of a set of specific directions for each title telling the analyst the issue, page, and specific BSUs on the page to be coded. To make locating BSUs efficient, Danielson and Mullen have created a plastic template marked off in the correct size.

On occasion, the selected BSU overlaps two types of content. In this instance, the investigator selects the content that constitutes more than half the BSU; or if it is evenly divided, he uses a random process to choose (flipping a coin perhaps). If the analyst is using a multiple coding system, the BSU can be double-coded.

Danielson and Mullen point out that it is important to remember that the BSU is only a *coding unit* in this process; the item (e.g., the article or advertisement) is still the *context unit* for coding purposes. Tests of the reliability and validity of the BSU have been made by researchers, and the results have been most encouraging. According to Danielson and Mullen, the disadvantages of the system are:

> 1/ Sample selection without the use of a computer is tedious.
> 2/ Because the coding unit differs from the context unit coders must be well-trained to avoid unreliability resulting from the misinterpretation of the context.
> 3/ There is likely to be some difficulty in coding units which overlap two or more content classifications.
> 4/ The method becomes inefficient if the study is limited to editorials, news pages, advertising, or any other type of content short of the total. It is also not useful in a search for infrequently occurring events or references or any specific questions such as, "Is source *X* favorably disposed toward concept *Y*?" [83, p. 110].

From the standpoint of theory, the researchers posed these questions.

> 1/ Is a *variable* unit really a unit?
> 2/ Newspaper content certainly is not randomly distributed on pages.

What influence will this have on sampling BSUs and on the total sampling error?

3/ What is the appropriate statistic for describing central tendency on a group of newspapers containing different numbers of BSUs—a weighted or unweighted average?

4/ When should proportionate sampling be used in newspaper content and when should disproportionate sampling be used.*

More study is needed in the area of sampling content to bring efficiency to content analysis as a research method and relieve the tedium of this research tool.

SUMMARY

Sampling can and usually should be employed in content analysis—and the procedures are not much different from those used in any other field of behavioral research. A number of studies have been conducted to determine adequacy of various sample sizes for the study of communication content, and, as was pointed out, the size of the sample is controlled to a great extent by the nature of the study. Data revealed through a sample are estimates of corresponding facts in the universe from which it was drawn. Steps can be taken to reduce errors in sampling—the most effective is to increase the sample size.

Sampling procedures that seem to be appropriate for use in content analysis include simple random sampling, stratified random sampling, interval sampling (with considerable caution), and cluster sampling. In practice, sampling in content analysis probably takes place at several different stages—most frequently when sampling titles, issues, and content. The analyst may find that he uses several sampling procedures at different times in an effort to obtain the final sample of content with which to work. Using several separate samplings on the same problem, by either the same or different methods, is referred to as multistage sampling and is very common in content analysis. Examples of purposive sampling were included, but as we have seen, the goals of purposive sampling can often be accomplished through stratification, thus strengthening the study considerably.

Regardless of the method used, no pat formula of application can be devised. The researcher must be thoroughly acquainted with his material and all of its peculiarities that might affect his sample design.

*Wayne Danielson and James Mullen, "A Basic Space Unit for Newspaper Content Analysis," paper presented at the Association for Education in Journalism Convention, Austin, Texas, 1964, pp. 9–10. [See 83 in bibliography.]

5

measurement

The assignment of numeric values to various characteristics of individuals, objects, or events through the use of a set of criteria is called *measurement*. Therefore its first requirement is the identification of the variable or variables under study. In behavioral research this is a matter of operational definition—intelligence as defined by linguistic and numeric skills, education by the number of years of formal schooling. In content analysis, categories such as subject matter or direction serve this function. When the variables are defined through an operational definition or set of definitions, the next step is to establish a system of observation. Systematic observation implies repeatability and reliability (discussed in Chapter 8). Lastly, a scheme must be devised for recording observations so that the data can be analyzed.

From another standpoint, measurement in the behavioral sciences is the key to validity. If the numeric weights imposed upon the characteristics being measured do not accurately represent real-world weights or relationships, the reconstructed reality in the form of numbers becomes a meaningless collection of data. There are four levels of measurement or scales with which the content analyst is concerned—nominal, ordinal, interval, and ratio—each arrived at by a different set of criteria for assigning numbers to the characteristics of objects.

The lowest level of measurement exists in the *nominal* (sometimes referred to as the classificatory) scale. Here, numbers or other symbols are used simply as a form of identifying an individual, object, or characteristic. Subject-matter categories, as they are employed in content analysis, are an example of the nominal level of measurement. They serve the same function as the names of diseases or the numbers assigned to participants in an athletic event. The name, label, or number attached to a category says only that the content classified under it differs from that placed in other categories. At the same time, the classes or categories in nominal measurement do not have a hierarchic or ordered structure, and the symbols assigned the categories may not be manipulated by the rules of arithmetic. Using nominal-scaling techniques, however, does permit you to describe certain group characteristics by counting the frequency of assignment of the category label to individuals or objects. The appropriate description of central tendency for such data measured in a nominal scale is the *mode*.

If you can determine that two objects not only are different but stand in some relative order to each other (i.e., one has more or less of a given quality than the other), you have an *ordinal* scale. For example, analysis of direction in content analysis constitutes an ordinal scale. Assume a directional analysis has three classifications: favorable (F), neutral (N), and unfavorable (U). In terms of favorability, the three classifications have an order that holds between all three pairs. If the symbol > stands for "more favorable than," F > N, N > U, and therefore, F > U. The order of the formal numbering system must be preserved when you assign ordinal scales to categories or objects. For example, if you wanted to assign scores to the three classifications above, F might equal 1, N equal 2, and U equal 3; or F equal 3, N equal 2, and U equal 1. So long as the numbering is consistent, it makes no difference whether the greater or the lesser quantity receives the highest score.

Although scoring in this manner is often and mistakenly treated as a precise set of scores, ordinal scales yield nothing more than a ranking of objects or characteristics. They provide no information on the magnitude of the differences between ranks. In classifying content as unfavorable, for example, some units will be more unfavorable than others and some perhaps, will be unfavorable to a degree only slightly less than neutral (a continuous variable).

In behavioral science, a great many scales measuring personality, attitude, or other factors are no more than ranking instruments or ordinal scales. As with the nominal scale, the rules of arithmetic do not apply to scores developed through ordinal-scaling methods. The appropriate measure of central tendency used in ordinal scaling is the *median*, since this statistic does not rely on the magnitude of the difference between scores but only on the number of scores above and below it.

When a scale provides all the information an ordinal scale provides and can also show the distance in units between any two scale points, it is said to be an *interval* scale. A very common interval scale is a thermometer. The units of measurement are constant, and the ratio between any two points on the scale can be computed without reference to the units of measurement or to a zero point (which is fixed arbitrarily in an interval scale). If all the characteristics of an interval scale are present plus an absolute zero point at the beginning (e.g., pounds, inches), the scale is called a *ratio* scale. All the operations of arithmetic are applicable to numbers assigned to objects on both interval and ratio scales.

Each of the four levels of measurement dictate certain kinds of statistical manipulation. Nominal and ordinal scales produce data that should, according to most statisticians, be analyzed by nonparametric statistical methods. In practice, however, behavioral-science data gathered through ordinal measurement have been analyzed using parametric statistics. Clearly, data gathered in interval and ratio scales may be analyzed by parametric statistical tests.

In content analysis, you will find that you will use all four levels of measurement—frequently at the same time. For example, a system of subject-matter categories represents nominal measurement. The establishment of direction categories for each subject-matter category represents ordinal measurement; and measurement of content may be made by a ratio scale (column inches, for example). A more detailed discussion of methods of analysis appropriate in content studies is the subject of Chapter 9.

UNITS OF MEASUREMENT

There are two basic units of measurement involved in content analysis. For the sake of consistency with other recent writings, we shall refer to them as the *coding unit* and the *context unit*. Note that what we call the coding unit subsumes both the recording unit and the enumeration unit defined by Berelson in his 1952 work.

CODING UNITS

The smallest segment of content counted and scored in content analysis is the coding unit. The most common coding units are a word; a theme or assertion; a paragraph; an item; a character, group, object, or institution; and space or time.

While counting specific *words* (for example, "democracy," "communism") is one of the easier forms of content analysis, it does not provide the analyst with as much information as some other methods. However, analysis of words does serve objectivity, since, at least denotatively, all the variations of a given word can be listed. A related discussion of symbol analysis appears in Chapter 6.

Sometimes the analyst finds that his material yields more information if he counts *assertions* or *themes* rather than words. Assertion or thematic analysis is, by its very nature, linked to direction categories. An assertion is a single thought unit or idea unit that conveys a single item of information extracted from a segment of content. An assertion could be a sentence, a part of a sentence, or even a single word. For example, the sentence "Alice is pretty" represents a single assertion. But in the sentence "Alice is an attractive, intelligent girl," there are three separate assertions: (1) Alice is attractive; (2) Alice is intelligent; and (3) Alice is a girl.

Both Yu [309] and Brown [284] give good explanations of their use of assertion analysis. For Brown, the theme was the unit of analysis. He counted assertions, specifying that a recurring similar assertion constituted a theme. Brown's Chapter 3 gives a step-by-step explanation of his procedure, with excerpts from his material to illustrate his methods of judging. Assertion analysis is discussed in greater detail in Chapter 6 of this book.

The *paragraph*, often used as a coding unit, causes problems when it contains more than one subject or more than one direction. This will be true to an even greater degree when *items* or whole *articles* are used to categorize content. Some studies use paragraphs as cues or indicators to classify entire items. For example, if the majority of paragraphs in an article can be classified in one subject-matter category or denotes one direction, the entire article is so classified. Using the entire article as the coding unit is acceptable when the project goals and the category system employed are of a general nature. If we are seeking to compare several newspapers or several news broadcasts merely for general content, such procedures would be workable. In such a situation, however, expect a lower index of agreement between coders than if the coding unit were a smaller segment of content. Paul Deutschmann developed a category system to overcome some of the difficulties that arise in coding. His procedure is discussed at length in Chapter 6.

The character is usually employed as a coding unit to find the answer to a highly specialized question—for example, how many times was Mr. X mentioned by name or by direct reference in an article, letter, or broadcast. It is probably more common to find the character serving as a referent or a category, in which all relevant information about a single character or character type (scientist, doctor, lawyer) is extracted from the content and subclassified under that heading. In these cases, some other unit, such as the theme or the word, serves as the actual coding unit. In one study, Hirsch [135] analyzed a random sample of magazine articles to determine the image of the scientist in science-fiction stories. Other studies have focused on the characterization of certain ethnic and cultural groups as represented in fiction, magazines, and other publications. Such work could be useful in subsequent studies involving stereotypes, for example. When the material has been gathered, any of a number of forms of analysis can be performed, e.g., thematic analysis, symbol analysis, evaluative-assertion analysis (discussed in Chapters 6 and 7). As was noted, in place of a character, the referent could be a group, an object, or an institution. The many studies of the image of the United States in the press of some other country are this type. The analyst separates and analyzes only news pertaining to the United States.

Among the more traditional methods of coding content are the space and time measurements, such as the column inch or minutes or seconds of broadcast time. The measures may be as gross as pages or whole issues of publications, depending on the statement of the problem. Such measurements are most tedious to execute, and for all the work, the researcher does not gain much insight into his materials. In addition, recent research has indicated that merely counting items produces results that correlate highly with the more laborious measuring of column inches (see Table 2).

Table 2/ Comparison of Three Content Measures Across Seventeen Subject-matter Categories in a Study of United States News in the Australian Press.

	r_{ca}*	r_{ci}*	r_{ai}*
New Zealand Herald	.98	.94	.96
Auckland Star	.96	.83	.89
Christchurch Star	.93	.91	.93
Dunedin Evening Star	.96	.94	.94
Sydney Daily Telegraph	.96	.92	.94
Sydney Sun	.98	.95	.95
Perth West Australian	.95	.94	.94
Hobart Mercury	.99	.96	.96

*c = column inches; *i* = item count; *a* = attention score

In many cases, several coding units are combined into an "attention score" or a "display index." Such indices quite often are more valuable than the simple measuring or counting procedures because they take into account more factors. Budd [62] described the use of an attention score that assigns points for various content features (e.g., multi-column headlines, position of the story on the page, column length of the article, page on which the article is located). This measure can overcome a situation in which several newspapers give approximately the same number of column inches to a subject (or a single publication to several subjects) but one gives it considerably stronger emphasis than do the others. The attention-score device correlates highly with item counts and measuring column inches. Table 2 shows coefficients derived from correlating seventeen subject-matter categories across three measures in eight newspapers [62].

From these data and those of other researchers [see particularly 7 and 140], it is clear that it is no longer necessary to measure column inches of content in descriptive studies; other and simpler means, the basic space unit described above, for example, serve as well.

THE CONTEXT UNIT

The context unit is the body of material surrounding the coding unit or, more precisely, as much of the material as is required to characterize the coding unit being analyzed. For example, if the coding unit is the word, the context unit may be the sentence in which the word appears – it might also be the paragraph or the entire article. The context unit needs to be large enough to provide the background necessary to permit accurate judging, but not so large that coders become confused.

In some instances, there may be both implicit and explicit context units. For example, the explicit context unit may be the article in which the coding unit appears. At the same time, the implicit coding unit may be the publication or publications analyzed. It is possible that a statement or assertion appearing in a labor-oriented publication may be coded favorable, but the same statement in a management-oriented publication be considered unfavorable.

METHODS IN MEASUREMENT AND RECORDING

In addition to choosing the units of analysis—coding and context—the analyst faces a number of other problems related to measurement. For example, if he is measuring column inches, does he count the space taken by the headline as well as by the text of the article? And what is the best method to record data in terms of efficiency of recording and subsequent analysis? How long does an article have to be before it qualifies as an item? Will he analyze content by one method and record by another (e.g., analyze direction on the basis of paragraphs, but record only entire articles)? What statistical tests will be used to analyze the data, and how will this affect measurement? Will he use a computer in the analysis of his data? These are only a few of the questions that must be answered before the actual analysis can be started. We shall attempt to answer some of the more general questions in this section, but basically it is a section for posing questions.

Since many analysts will undoubtedly continue to measure column inches, we shall consider that first. Do you include the measurement of the headline in accounting for space? The reasoning seems to be that the headline is an integral part of the story, probably has high impact, and may influence to a great extent the manner in which the story is read. If we do not measure this space, how do we account for it? Relegate it to a miscellaneous category? This question becomes important when we are looking at data in terms of the news hole—the part of the newspaper or magazine devoted to news as opposed to advertising. Headlines take up a great deal of space and should be included in measurement unless there is a very good reason for excluding them.

Is it necessary to measure space to the nearest quarter-inch? Probably measuring to even the nearest half-inch confers a false notion of rigor that is not warranted by most content studies. You will recall that measurements as gross as the item correlate quite highly with the most painstaking column-inch measurements. Many analysts have also been overly concerned about column width and slavishly convert odd-sized columns to a standard width for recording purposes. This problem can be avoided if findings are expressed in relation to a standard news hole. Using the news hole also solves the problem of comparing tabloids with standard-size newspapers. But all these complications seem hardly worth the effort and could be entirely eliminated by simply counting items.

A great deal of time can be saved in most content studies if the method of recording data is chosen while the method that will be used to analyze it is kept in mind. If, for example, you intend to use a computer to analyze your data, you should devise a recording scheme that allows direct punching of data cards from the tabulations. Coding sheets specifically designed for this purpose are available at most computer centers (see Chapter 10).

If you plan to do the analysis by hand, a number of possibilities are available. In his study of news of the United States in the press "down-under," Budd [63] used 4- by 6-inch cards printed especially for his purposes. They were designed so that he could easily record the headline width in columns, subject-matter category, direction, column inches of the news story or other item, position on the page, type of item, summary of the article's content, date of the newspaper, source of the story, and page on which it appeared. Each completed card represented one item, and a different color card was used for each publication. Budd was able to sort his data cards by direction and category, compute his attention score, and make other computations by calculator quite rapidly.

Another possibility is the tabular or columnar pad, which comes in a variety of sizes for accounting purposes. Peterson and Thorp [195] used a standard thirteen-column pad, with space in the left-hand margin in which to write the name of each newspaper. For the authors' purposes, each column was divided in half, one side to record an editorial's length, the other for coding subject-matter category. These pads were useful in three ways: the total space devoted to editorials in each category could be computed quickly, without having to handle hundreds of cards; a count could be made quickly of how many newspapers carried editorials and of how many issues contained editorials. Further, data from the columnar pad is easily converted into tables to accompany the reports of the research.

Still another alternative is provided by the McBee keysort system, which uses cards punched and sorted by hand. A coding system can be devised to correspond to sequential series of numbers around the four sides of the card. Each card can be punched with a hand punch and later sorted with an instrument that resembles an ice pick. One advantage of this method is that it is relatively inexpensive. A broader discussion of keysort processing can be found in Goode and Hatt [16].

Finally, quantification in content analysis, as in other research, leads eventually to summarizing procedures resulting in some sacrifice of detail. Frequencies and column inches are summarized in tables as averages or percentages or are transformed into indices or attention scores to be used as a single variable in subsequent analysis. The individual case is lost in summarizing the data. What is gained is, of course, more valuable. For the analyst in reality has lost nothing by summarizing—by his quantification procedures. He has traded some unmanageable data for manageable information; he has exchanged his individual data for general answers, efficiency, and scientific rigor. If the analyst has not made these trades, his measurement was in vain, and he might just as well have given his material an armchair reading.

Two other important phases of measurement in content analysis—categories and direction—have only been mentioned in this chapter. Because of their complexities, the next two chapters are devoted to them.

6

categories

No content analysis is better than its categories, for a system or set of categories is, in essence, a conceptual scheme. Where categories are in fact variables, they are linked to the problem and the theories on which the research is based. Further, categories differentiate and describe the content being investigated – in newspapers, magazines, radio or television broadcasts, cartoons, or documents – and form a crucial link between the actual counting or measuring and the larger fields of theory and concept. These categories are not mere labels, but compartments with explicitly defined boundaries into which material is grouped for analysis.

The analyst looks for classification cues (categories) in the nature of the research problem itself, the specific hypotheses formulated or questions to be answered (the goals of the study), the content to be analyzed, and the type of analysis that is selected. The analyst develops his categories within the framework of three primary requirements. Categories must accurately fit the needs of the study so that they answer the questions originally asked, be exhaustive (relative to the problem), and be mutually exclusive. (See the discussion of the Deutschmann study and facet analysis in Chapter 9 for a solution to the often vexing problem of mutual exclusiveness.)

DEVELOPING CATEGORIES

To learn how to develop content categories within the broad rules stated, the beginning content analyst might look for an example to the methods used by Donohew [288] in his study of Medicare news. Donohew knew that the content of the newspapers he was analyzing would fall into one of three direction categories: favorable to Medicare, unfavorable, or neutral. Therefore, one major problem was to develop categories that would accurately reflect content direction. These categories would provide answers to basic questions Donohew was asking about the relationship of certain environmental forces to the gatekeeping activities of wire editors. The category system—direction and content—had to provide data for correlation analysis with community variables (the environmental forces) such as the publisher's attitude toward Medicare, the perceived attitude of the community, and the percent of the community over age sixty-five. The final analyses were to provide tests of hypotheses centered on the basic question underlying the research: What forces in the communication channel (newspapers) determine what is said about an issue (Medicare bill before Congress)?

The content and its form provided answers to some of the technical questions. Most of the content was news stories, some was editorials, and a smaller amount was editorial cartoons. Editorials and cartoons were classified by direction after inspection only, without an elaborate system of categories; the entire editorial (or cartoon) was the unit. News stories usually have short paragraphs, each devoted to a single theme; preliminary reading disclosed the major theses (categories), and a coding sheet was constructed (see Figure 4).

Examination of the coding sheet shows that it provides answers to the major questions asked of the content and therefore is suitable for the content under study, that the categories are exhaustive (any content unsuitable for listed categories could be noted in the Other Themes section), and that the categories are mutually exclusive. Each content item (e.g., news story) was given a net score, and net scores were used in the computation of canonical correlations with other variables.

Because the Medicare study was primarily a directional study, elaborate content categories were developed to minimize coder bias, a major stumbling block in directional analysis. When the coder read a newspaper paragraph and placed it in the proper content category, the paragraph was simultaneously placed in the proper direction category, thus considerably reducing the problem of subjective judgment. A paragraph that did not contain statements predominantly in one direction or the other was placed in the neutral (balanced) category. A paragraph with two or more statements in the same direction was assigned to a general category broad enough to cover both statements. But the important bit of information – direction – remained unchanged.

In addition to specific examples, a few general remarks on developing categories may be useful. Content analysis begins with the research

Newspaper: *Date:* *Story Source:*

–		+	
Expressions of opposition to Medicare		Expressions favoring Medicare	
Actions in opposition to Medicare		Actions in support of Medicare	
Statements supporting opponents of Medicare		Statement attacking opponents of Medicare	
Statements attacking proponents of Medicare		Statements supporting proponents of Medicare	
Statements listing opponents of Medicare		Statements listing proponents of Medicare	
Bill not likely to pass		Bill likely to pass	
Alternate plan or amendment sought by opposition		Actions opposing alternate plan	
Provisions of alternate plan		Statements opposing alternate plan	
Opposition amendment approved		Opposition amendment defeated	
Some other plan (e.g. Kerr-Mills) satisfactory		President insists on Social Security plan	
Effects of defeat on other measures – harmful		Effects of passage on other bills – helpful	
Effects of defeat praised by opposition		Effects of defeat of bill called harmful	
Provisions of original plan – costs		Provisions of original plan – benefits	
Opponents may delay vote		Proponents press for vote	
Miscellaneous –		Miscellaneous +	

0		*Other themes*	
Bill approaches vote			
Vote on Medicare to be close			
What will happen to it if passes/fails Senate			
Possible areas of compromise			
Miscellaneous			

CONTENT TOTALS	HEADLINE	HEADLINE CONTENT (+1, –1, or 0)	EDITORIAL OR EDITORIAL CARTOON (+1, –1, or 0)
+ ______	Head size ______		
– ______	Location on page ______		
0 ______	Length ______		
Net ______	Total score and direction ______		

Figure 4/ Coding sheet used in Donohew's study of Medicare.

problem, and the nature of the problem should suggest one of the analyst's first questions: What classification would most efficiently yield the data needed to satisfy the problem's demands? That is, the analyst first looks for cues to category development in the nature of the problem itself.

You may be chiefly interested in content characteristics (e.g., symbols of democracy), what the content reveals about its producer or its causes (Copperhead themes in Northern editorials), what the content indicates about the source's perceptions of his audience, or the possible effect of the content on the audience. (With the last type of study, the analyst must proceed with caution. To determine effects, he must study the content and the audience.) In any case, the answers you seek should be the first determinant of the system of categories you use, because categories are the counterparts of the questions normally asked in any research study.

Political content analysis illustrates this point. As part of an analysis of the Nixon-Douglas campaign, Bush [65] used these fairly standard categories, each listed as one of his propaganda themes: personal traits ("personal virtues of the candidates, and political morality"), campaign issues (e.g., "national security"), and candidates' positions on issues (direction categories). Traits, issues, and positions fitted the nature and purposes of the Bush study: "To describe the content in terms of propaganda themes used by each candidate and his supporters" and "to measure the direction of such news."

The second source of cues to category development relates content categories to research hypotheses or goals. Although much of the literature of content analysis gives no indication that hypotheses were formulated and tested, research goals are frequently stated and findings are presented within the goals' framework. In some studies there may be too little theoretical basis or previous research to formulate meaningful hypotheses; in these cases pointed questions or propositions may be more useful. However, scientific hypotheses state expected relationships between variables and should help to focus the research on the crucial parts of the problem. Categories specify the data; and statistical operations on the data are the mechanisms to test the hypotheses, the expected relationships.

> The hypotheses derive from the nature of the problem and in a sense help to refine it. The general categories for analysis are contained in the hypotheses and they in turn are translated into concrete, specific indicators for purposes of actual analysis. The actual results are then generalized and applied to the level of the categories and thus constitute a test of the hypotheses under investigation [2, pp. 164–165].

Indicators, or indicants, may be considered almost as subcategories; their function is to point out a characteristic that is not, itself, measurable. Cartwright [7] likened indicators to the "operational definition of a category." Thus, in determining the bias (or fairness) of newspapers in an election campaign, Klein and Maccoby [150] measured for each newspaper in the sample the number and length of stories about each candidate, size of headlines, direction of headlines, and number and size of pictures. These indicators were examined within the framework of each newspaper's editorial position to see if that position influenced the coverage given each candidate. Stoodley [234] envisioned integrity as a continuum with indicators of honesty, fairness, and impartiality, and their negative counterparts, and he counted instances of these in newspaper content relating to a Federal Communications Commission investigation.

The use of indicators in content analysis is, therefore, similar to their use in attitude measurement (which content analysis sometimes attempts). The psychologist uses a test to measure an attitude, or he may observe his subject's behavior and make a judgment about the presence or absence of the attitude; but the attitude is a construct — "an invented name for a property," as Kerlinger says [21, p. 418]. Similarly, the content analyst observes communication behavior, in the form of his content, and tries to determine the source's attitude(s) toward some object.

Indicators are used frequently with theme categories. For example, one major theme derived from Nazi propaganda was "The United States is internally corrupt." This attitude-theme was indicated by statements about "political and economic injustice, war profiteering, plutocratic exploitation, Communist sedition, Jewish conspiracy, and spiritual decay" [23, p. 180].

Thus far, our discussion of category development has focused on studies of limited subject matter, such as Medicare. Content analyses of broader scope — e.g., the total nonadvertising content of a newspaper — present different problems. These will be discussed in relation to the three primary requirements for categories outlined above, using the Deutschmann study [11] of twelve daily newspapers for examples.

Deutschmann's purposes were "to demonstate in a number of *quantitative* ways the nature of the *qualitative* differences" in the papers' contents and, he hoped, "to say something about what content 'normally' is composed of" in the dozen papers. Content categories were based on the fifty-category list developed at Stanford [see Bush, 66]; ten basic categories with forty-nine subcategories were used. The study was further organized on the newsroom dimensions of the content items: form — e.g., (type, chart); geographic origin and relation to reader; when — (e.g., daily story, regular feature), and who — what kinds of persons the items discussed. The content categories were, in newsroom terminology, "what the story was about."

The Deutschmann study fulfilled the first requirement and avoided a pitfall in developing content categories – excessive fractionation, that is, more categories than needed to answer the questions. In one category where two subcategories proved impractical, they were combined into one. Combining categories after coding can be done, but dividing a category after coding is almost always impossible. Hence, the opposite of excessive categories – too few to provide the information needed – is a shortcoming impossible to overcome under most coding schemes. The solution to the problem of determining the right number of categories lies in careful design of the study, pointed answers to the standard what-do-I-want-to-know question, preliminary study of samples of content, and some practice coding of the content to test the category system.

> Categories should, therefore, be added only when they bear upon the hypotheses being tested. The purpose of elaborate preliminary examination of every possible complication is not to incorporate all of them in the schemes but rather to find the simplest schemes which will yield the data wanted [24, p. 52].

In trying to make category systems exhaustive, many analysts have found it both necessary and desirable to include a category labeled miscellaneous. Perhaps it is unrealistic to expect every item to fit into at least one of the major categories designed. In fact, to fit an item into a category where it does not rightly belong injects error into the findings. However, the miscellaneous classification must be used with discretion. It is altogether too easy to cast an item (sentence, paragraph, article) into this category when, with a little more thought, it might be placed under its proper heading. Although the miscellaneous category is a valid classification for content, the category generally should account for only a small percentage of all the material analyzed.

Concerning the third primary requirement, categories are mutually exclusive if there is only one proper place for each item (although as we shall see, a most acceptable deviation from this principle has been developed by Deutschmann). This means that every subject category must be completely and thoroughly defined, indicating what type of material is and is not to be included. It is imperative that such definitions be written down before coding begins. Furthermore, because it is virtually impossible to anticipate every situation that will arise during coding, each category definition should allow for expansion (addition to the definition) or logical extension (implicit allowance for unanticipated cases).

An unanticipated case caused Budd [63], for example, to redefine one category in his study of news about the United States carried by Australian and New Zealand newspapers. An item concerning a vacation trip of an American politician's wife did not fit under the definition for Diplomacy and Foreign Relations or under Prominent Individuals until the latter category was extended to include "dependents of political personages involved in nongovernmental or nonpolitical activities." The extension also allowed for any additional items of the same nature.

The three requirements for content categories—that they be appropriate, exhaustive, and mutually exclusive—are especially crucial to reliability and validity, discussed in Chapter 8. It was reliability—coding reliability—that induced Deutschmann to depart from the principle of mutually exclusive categories.

> An exceedingly large number of newspaper items are complex. You can hardly begin to say "what" they are about, if you are restricted to only one category.
>
> As a compromise procedure, we instructed our coders to use two codes whenever they felt it was necessary. Further, we said to attach no significance to the order of coding, but rather put down the two content codes which *best* describe the story [11, p. 63].

Double-coding raised coder agreement from 70 per cent to over 90 per cent. While double-coding can produce sums over 100 per cent, that disadvantage is offset by the reliable information about "the relative *emphasis* given to a kind of content" [11, p. 64].

The examples cited should make clear that there is no single best way of developing a set of categories to reveal the characteristics of all forms of content. Most of the literature on content analysis bears this out, although several analysts would prefer a greater degree of standardization. Lasswell, perhaps because he has concentrated on propaganda analysis through symbol coding, is one who has argued for a single system of categories that could be generally applied. The argument against the single system is that each content analysis is unique, presenting individual problems that require individual handling. To reiterate our position: Each study must be designed primarily on the basis of its purpose and the type of content involved.

Much information on subject-matter categories can be gathered by skimming the articles in the bibliography. Of these articles, however, only Bush's [66] directly attacks the problem of categories for general news content. The Bush article is notable because it lists fifty possible categories, each of which is defined in specific terms. Bush's list lends itself to expansion or condensation, and the definitions can be readily altered to fit any study. Budd [63], in his study of the Australian and New Zealand press, used the Bush list as a basis for devising seventeen subject categories for general news content. Deutschmann's modification has already been cited. Cutlip [79] also lists a number of subject-matter categories in his study of the flow of Associated Press news, although he does not offer category definitions in his article.

Often overlooked is the fact that what is *not* published in a given medium may be as important as – if not more important than – what *is* published. Lewis [162] deals peripherally with this in his study of United States newspapers' coverage of the Cuban revolution. Martin and Nelson [172] also provide some methodological guidance in this area.

Aside from subject-matter and direction categories, Berelson [2] lists several other types:

1. *Standards* or *grounds* refer to the bases (or grounds) on which classification of direction was made. These categories are used concurrently with direction categories. Analyses of this type generally center around the analysis of key symbols or words that classify an article as either favorable or unfavorable, etc. This system was used by Lasswell, Lerner, and Pool [24] in the RADIR studies.

2. *Values* describe belief systems or goals – "What are the communicators after?" Such categories are expected to uncover the goals that are explicitly or implicitly contained in the communications content. This type of category is most often used in analyses of fiction but is adaptable to studies of nonfiction. Value categories have been used extensively in propaganda analysis and the analysis of political campaign speeches. Chapters 9 and 10 in Lasswell et al [23] should prove helpful to the reader interested in values as content categories. Albrecht's study [42] of common values in literature will also he helpful.

3. The *origin* or *incidence* category, according to Berelson, "is sometimes relevant in indicating how widely or narrowly the audience's attention is being directed" [2, p. 158]. For example, a study of the South American press [169] indicates that a high proportion of its foreign news is provided by the French news agency Agence France-Presse. This might indicate that readers in South America are not receiving the same version of world events as those in the United States. (Content analysis could test this proposition of course.)

Another approach is the geographic category–grouping items on the basis of their geographic origin, usually determined by dateline [169]. Deutschmann [11] used point-of-origin categories, but in a second grouping of data he took undatelined (local) stories and classified each according to the content's geographic relationship to the local reader. Thus a locally written interview with a foreign dignitary, for example, would be reclassified as foreign. This reanalysis caused some shifting in percentages among the local, national, and foreign categories.

A number of what-is-said categories are possible. They include methods or actions, usually used in conjunction with values, traits, or abilities. Methods and actions may be indicators that the actor holds certain values; abilities describe characteristics of persons in the communication. Other what-is-said categories are actor categories, to reveal in whose name statements are made, and target-addressee categories to classify communication content by its destination. The last type of category may involve a shift of focus from sender or message to the audience, or it may be designed to reveal the communicator's beliefs about his audience's characteristics. Bush [66] classified items according to Nature of the Central Person and a variation of this scheme was used by Deutschmann [11].

As we have seen, categories deriving from *content* – i.e., dealing with what is said—are divided into subject matter and direction. (Chapter 7 deals extensively with classification of direction.) Categories may also be derived from the *form* of the content—the way in which a particular body of content is structured, i.e., how it is said.

Other useful categories include *type of statement* (e.g., news, editorial, fiction, or nonfiction), a gross category usually used as a framework for further classification; *form of statement*, sentence-by-sentence analysis to describe grammatical or syntactical form; and *intensity* (more fully discussed in Chapter 7) to indicate strength or excitement value. Intensity analysis may be used to test differences between sources or contents and is valuable because intensity (or emphasis or strength) of material is supposed to have an effect on readers.

Other category schemes include time—1940 to 1945, June to December, 6 to 10 P.M.; typographical emphasis – size of headline, position, length of item; or, much broader, *relevance* and *nonrelevance*. Gerbner [108] used two broad categories, *substantive* and *procedural*, to describe Yugoslavian and United States headlines for stories about the United Nations. Budd [63] employed *substantively oriented* and *socially oriented* categories to identify content type in a study of foreign publications.

The important point to remember is that the categories should be chosen according to the nature of the content, the research problem and its goals, and the hypotheses to be tested.

THEMATIC ANALYSIS

One special kind of content category is the *theme category*. Whereas the theme itself is considered a unit of analysis, each theme detected is placed in a larger "compartment" known as a theme category. A variety of different themes with essentially the same basic meaning can be classified under a single theme category. "A theme is an assertion about a subject matter" [2, p. 18]; the subject is a *referent* (e.g., the United States, Stalin, British foreign policy) and must be present or implied in the assertion.

Themes are derived from content, but their categories need not be if an appropriate category system is available. The nature of the problem and the available resources determine the decision. Lasswell [23], in a statement analysis of an American periodical, searched for assertions consistent with or contradictory to Nazi propaganda themes already extracted from German broadcasts monitored by the Federal Communications Commission. The analysis compared the content of a known propaganda channel with that of a magazine whose publisher was under indictment for sedition. The Nazi themes served as categories, and each occurrence of a theme in the American publication was coded and counted to provide a frequency distribution.

One theme derived from Nazi broadcasts was: The United States is weak (an assertion about the United States). Any statement in the American publication asserting United States weakness, for example, in materials, manpower, morale, was coded into this category. The following statement was placed in the America-is-weak category:

> Meanwhile, fighting the whole universe goes on, and the morale of the American people threatens to go so low that they must stand on a sheet of paper to look into the eyes of a mouse [23, p. 184].

Statements contradicting the theme also were recorded, to provide a ratio of consistency and contradiction. In a similar case, Lasswell [23] drew four propaganda aims from public pronouncements of Nazi officials and used them as theme categories in analyzing two American publications.

In developing theme categories, therefore, the analyst must be able to detect the major motifs in the content and recognize them in their various statement forms.

The referent is the key to category development in thematic analysis, as shown in Brown's study [284] of anti-Catholic campaign literature. He classified eighteen recurring themes under only four theme categories; each was a referent, a target of the content: the Roman Catholic Church, the Pope, Roman Catholics, and John F. Kennedy. Brown defined a theme as:

> . . . the plural of assertion. A single statement of meaning is an assertion. When that assertion recurs, it is called a theme. (It isn't necessary for exactly the same assertion to recur . . . assertions, which carry the same essential meaning, although they may be slightly different, have a common theme.)
>
> In all cases, assertions are homogeneously arranged into themes. In this way, a theme may contain a minimum of two assertions having the same essential meaning [284, p. 15].

A single sentence could contain several assertions, all classifiable under a single theme (anti-Roman Catholics, for example) or each classifiable under separate themes. If a sentence contained separate items of information, Brown treated the content as separate assertions. For example, from the sentence "Lincoln, Garfield and McKinley were assassinated by Roman Catholics . . . ; Theodore Roosevelt was shot and wounded by a Roman Catholic . . . ," Brown extracted four assertions:

1/ Lincoln was assassinated by Roman Catholics.
2/ Garfield was assassinated by Roman Catholics.
3/ McKinley was assassinated by Roman Catholics.
4/ Roosevelt was wounded by a Roman Catholic.

Brown classified these as anti-Catholic assertions on the same theme – "that of Catholics assassinating or attempting to assassinate."

To devise realistic, discriminating themes and theme categories, Brown did a pilot study in which he searched each document "for assertions which appeared to be anti-Catholic or anti-anything related to the Roman Catholic Church, including John Kennedy." Each assertion was listed on a separate sheet of paper; examination and sorting of assertions indicated that the targets were logical theme categories.

Targets of the propaganda served as subjects of each theme Brown formulated to use in classifying the material. For example, Brown derived this theme from the content:

> Is (are) powerful, treacherous, ruthless, conspiring, insidious, deceiving, bribe(s), lie(s) [284, p. 48].

If any of the targets was the subject of a statement making an assertion such as "It lies," the coder put it into the proper target-theme category where it could be subjected to frequency-distribution and other analyses.

7

direction

Determination of direction in content analysis is probably one of the most frustrating problems facing the researcher, because it is one area in which the element of subjectivity is difficult to control and impossible to eliminate entirely. At the same time, content analysis can be most productive when it is able to show direction—or the lack of it.

DIRECTION DEFINED

Concerning direction, Berelson wrote:

> Although direction is a commonly recognized characteristic of communication content, it is not always easily analyzed in an objective fashion. Many textual passages are not clearly pro or con or neutral; the borderline is often indistinct [2, p. 150].

According to Lasswell, Lerner, and Pool [24] direction in content analysis refers to the "attitude expressed toward any symbol by its user." But the content analyst has no way of knowing what attitude the writer of a communication intended to convey. Expressions of attitude are usually categorized by the analyst as favorable or unfavorable, with different writers using different labels for these categories: pro-con, positive-negative, friendly-hostile, indulgence-deprivation, approval-disapproval, optimistic-pessimistic, relief-discomfort, consonance-dissonance, affirmative-negative, to mention a few. Generally, all these pairs include a third category, neutral, and the recording operations usually involve the assignment of a plus, zero, or minus to designate the category. It should be noted that other writers have used different terms for "direction," e.g., orientation (Allport and Faden), character (Harris and Lewis). For the sake of consistency, and because it is the term most commonly used, "direction" will be used throughout this chapter.

DETERMINING DIRECTION

The scheme for quantifying direction that is eventually established should not be designed before the material has been examined. The analyst should become thoroughly familiar with the material to be analyzed and should determine the modes to be employed for revealing a given stand on an issue. Only when this familiarization process is complete can the researchers determine an effective scheme (including definitions) for classifying and counting direction.

What kinds of references are favorable or unfavorable? This is generally a matter of definition. It is the responsibility of the analyst to formulate complete and logical definitions of favorable and unfavorable material—definitions that clarify what each category does and does not include. The more precise and complete the definitions are, the easier the job of coding and classifying the data will be. Although such definitions are somewhat subjective, they tell the reader of the study how the final figures were obtained. Further, because many criteria and procedures used in the classification of direction are necessarily based on knowledge of outside events and expected audience responses, the researcher should include such criteria in his definitions.

A common pitfall in classifying direction is the tendency to isolate symbols and to equate them with a direction without reference to their context. Lasswell, Lerner, and Pool point out: "There is almost no theory of language which predicts the specific words one will emit in the course of expressing the contents of his thoughts. The content analyst, therefore, does not know what to expect" [24, p. 49]. Many errors appear in the results of content analyses because the method employed was based on an inadequate concept of the language of the material. To account for context, the standards of favorableness and unfavorableness must be sensitive to the meaning of the content rather than merely the isolated set of symbols. For example, assume that strength is adjudged a characteristic favorable to labor. Rigidly applying this rule the statement, "Jimmy Hoffa is so powerful that he could cripple American industry and inflict heavy damage on the United States economy" would have to be judged as favorable. However, the context in which the word powerful (denoting strength) appeared might not be considered one that is favorable to labor.

When the analyst has drawn up a set of preliminary rules for classifying direction, his next step is to conduct a pilot study on the material to be analyzed. In doing this, he need not worry about drawing a scientifically representative sample of the material with which to work, although he should draw it, informally, so that it will be as heterogeneous as possible with respect to the things he is assessing. A selection of several issues or a number of broadcast scripts would serve the purpose. In a pilot study, the researcher will probably not meet all the problems he will face during the analysis proper, but it will be most unusual if, as a result of such a study, he does not make some revision in his direction-category definitions. The pilot study will also indicate whether the prescribed coding and recording system (discussed elsewhere in this book) are functioning properly and may suggest changes or alterations in the initial plan.

It is also profitable to subject definitions and devices for the classification and recording of direction to an objectivity or reliability test. This means allowing a *number* of coders to apply the techniques to the material intended for analysis. The degree of agreement between the analyst's own work and the work of a panel of others may give an indication of the reliability of the measuring devices. Reliability tests will be discussed at length in Chapter 8.

Usually, the content analyst confronts two major problems in seeking to determine direction. One is the question of how complete he needs to be; the second is the issue of how objective he can be. To judge how precise his quantification must be, the analyst should consider the use to which his findings will be put and the extent to which a small difference in percentages will influence the way the problem will be treated.

Gieber, in a study of the relative amount of negative news published by daily newspapers, evolved a good negative-positive scheme of classifying content which offers both simplicity and completeness.

Negative—those items that report social conflicts and disorganization:

1/ International tension: conflict between nations – military, political, and economic.
2/ Civil disruption: conflict between groups – political, economic, and social.
3/ Crime and vice.
4/ Accidents and disasters.

Positive – those items reflecting social cohesion and cooperation:

1/ International cooperation: normal communications among nations.
2/ Government at work: information (noncontroversial) on affairs of government.
3/ Society at work: information about the groups of persons cooperating in nongovernmental affairs.
4/ "Life Goes On": news items about individuals [110, pp. 311-312].

Gieber's definitions include certain subject categories, such as crime and accidents, only under the negative classification. From a different point of view, one might be able to classify certain articles concerning crime as positive news, for example, a dramatic reduction in the rate of crime. As previously stated, direction-category definitions must be adaptable enough to account for such an interpretation.

It is obvious, therefore, that to account for every possible situation that might arise in the classification of direction, category definitions would have to be unmanageably large. To be useful, definitions of direction must be broad enough in scope to cover almost every situation that might arise but not so general that they fail to provide the desired discrimination. Such definitions operate as a frame of reference within which the researcher can work. Cony [74], in a study similar to Gieber's but published earlier, established more adaptable definitions to analyze conflict-cooperation content in daily newspapers. Cony points out, however, that his coders were required to exercise subjective judgment in a small number of cases. Budd employed the Gieber definitions as a base but expanded the definitions as criteria for judging news as favorable, unfavorable, or neutral.

> *Favorable:* Those items reflecting social cohesion and cooperation and political and economic stability and/or strength. Favorability will be judged on the basis of international cooperation (political, social and economic) in which the United States, or any group or individual representing the United States, is depicted as strong, right or cooperative. In internal affairs, favorability will be judged on the basis of persons cooperating in political, social and economic affairs. For example, events and incidents which depict the United States, or any group or individual within the United States as progressive, successful, peace-loving, moral, intelligent, lawful, unified or as exercising leadership will be considered favorable. This classification will not be assigned where the United States, or any group or individual thereof, is depicted as exploiting its strength upon weaker nations, groups or individuals.
>
> *Unfavorable:* Those items which report social conflict and disorganization and political and economic instability and/or weakness. Unfavorability will be judged on the basis of international tensions (political, social and economic) in which the United States, or any group or individual representing the United States, is depicted as weak, wrong or uncooperative. In internal affairs, unfavorability will be judged on the basis of civil disruption in which there is conflict between persons or groups of persons within the United States in political, economic or social affairs. For example, events and incidents which depict the United States, or any group or individual within the United States, as backward, domineering, immoral, impractical, unlawful, disunified or lacking in leadership will be classified unfavorable.
>
> *Neutral:* Those items which reflect neither favorable or unfavorable conditions either through balance of content or a lack of controversial material [285, pp. 83-84].

Bush [65] designed direction categories to quantify political campaign news as favorable or unfavorable. To try to eliminate the subjective element, Bush established a list of prearranged additional criteria for classifying specific cases not covered by the basic scheme for determining direction.

The Bush study suggests another procedure that can be used in writing definitions for direction categories. It is neither unethical nor unscientific to expand definitions of direction as new developments occur and after the study is under way. If the analyst encounters a statement, paragraph, or article, etc., that cannot be classified because the original rules do not provide for it, he can refine his rules so that the statement can be classified. However, if the researcher does extend his rules in this way, he must make certain that he has not previously classified a similar statement in some other manner. The analyst will find it worthwhile to make immediate note of any changes he makes in classification procedure during the course of the analysis. If the study in which the researcher is engaged is a comparative study, he has the added responsibility of ensuring that the rules applied to one publication (or outlet) are consistent with those applied in the analysis of the other outlets with which he will be drawing comparisons.

EXPANDED DIRECTIONAL ANALYSIS

Many analysts have gone beyond the two and three-category models of directional analysis. Joseph Tabak [304], analyzing *United States News and World Report* during the 1960 election campaign, employed four directional categories. In addition to favorable, unfavorable, and neutral, he used a "balanced" category. Tabak felt the balanced category was necessary to classify content that was a combination of favorable and unfavorable material. While he thought a combination of favorable and unfavorable material might have a neutralizing effect on the reader of *U.S. News*, he felt the balanced category would give a more complete picture of the magazine's content. Kaplan and Goldsen,* in a study of wartime communications, defined several levels of direction, as follows:

1/ *Unqualified Positive* (+ +): Favorable presentation of the symbol, without explicit qualification of its favorable character.
2/ *Qualified Positive* (− +): A basically favorable presentation, with unfavorable aspects clearly involved.

*The direction classifications outlined by Kaplan and Goldsen are described in detail in Documents 40 and 41, Experimental Division for the Study of Wartime Communications, Library of Congress.

3/ *Unqualified Negative* (– –): Unqualified unfavorable presentation.
4/ *Qualified Negative* (+ –): Basically unfavorable, with favorable or ameliorating aspects clearly involved.
5/ *Balanced* (±): Both favorable and unfavorable presentations clearly and equally involved.
6/ *No Direction* (0) : Presentations involving neither favorable nor unfavorable aspects (often called neutral) [23, p. 97].

Even more complex schemes have been developed to get at direction of content. For example, several studies have classified direction within direction. One such study [26] first analyzed radio, newspaper, and magazine content as pro-Democratic or pro-Republican; then the material under each heading was classified according to whether it was for that party's own candidate or against the opposing candidate. If we use the 1960 election campaign to illustrate the procedure, material that was classified pro-Democratic could have been either pro-Kennedy or anti-Nixon. Another study [300] of the 1960 election news used a similar approach but devised eleven directional categories, allowing news favorable to one party or the other but unfavorable to that party's candidate, or unfavorable to the party but favorable to the candidate, or unfavorable to the candidate and unfavorable to the party, and so on. The categories were coded +D-K, –D+K, –D-K.

The complexities of such directional categories should be in keeping with the purpose of the study, i.e., the use to which the findings will be put. It is highly possible that the use of too many directional categories could obscure a meaningful analysis of direction. In the same vein, if the analyst is employing a sample of content, excessive fragmentation will result in fewer items in each classification, thus reducing the reliability of the results as well as limiting the possibilities of statistical tests.

In studies where the classification of direction can be reduced to terms of favorable and unfavorable content, an overall estimate of the degree of imbalance has been developed. Imbalance pertains to the extent of differences in the ratios of favorable, neutral, and unfavorable material accorded to the topic or symbol under analysis. Janis and Fadner [23, Ch. 8] have evolved a statistical concept for measuring imbalance called the coefficient of imbalance. The coefficient, which appears not to have had wide use, is designed so that it will always:

1/ Increase in the positive direction when the frequency of units of favorable content increases.
2/ Increase in the negative direction when the frequency of units of unfavorable content increases.
3/ Equal zero if all the units of content are neutral or if there is no relevant content.
4/ Equal zero if the number of units of favorable content are equal to the number of units of unfavorable content.

The authors say that their coefficient can be applied to any type of communication provided it can be classified into the categories of favorable, unfavorable, and neutral content. The coefficient, by definition, provides a single figure which shows the relationship between favorable and unfavorable material. Since the figure is computed on the basis of the total relevant content for each publication (or radio or television broadcast), it can be used to make direct comparisons with other media. The statistical formulas necessary to compute the coefficient of imbalance are as follows [23, p. 169]:

$$C_f = \frac{f^2 - fu}{rt} \qquad f > u$$

$$C_u = \frac{fu - u^2}{rt} \qquad f < u$$

Where f = favorable units of content
u = unfavorable units of content
t = number of units of total content
r = total units of relevant content

Note that r = favorable + unfavorable + neutral units of content
t = favorable + unfavorable + neutral + nonrelevant units of content

For purposes of illustration, assume you have a total of 80 paragraphs of content, all of them relevant to the issue under study. Of the total, 70 paragraphs are classified favorable and 10 paragraphs unfavorable. Since $f > u$, we employ

$$C_f = \frac{f^2 - fu}{rt}$$

Substituting $$C_f = \frac{70^2 - 70 \cdot 10}{80 \cdot 80} = \frac{4{,}200}{6{,}400} = .66$$

If you have a total of 100 units, 70 favorable, 10 unfavorable, 10 neutral, and 10 nonrelevant, the coefficient is developed as follows.

Substituting $$C_f = \frac{70^2 - 70 \cdot 10}{90 \cdot 100} = \frac{4{,}200}{9{,}000} = .47$$

Batlin, in a study of the 1952 election campaign coverage, employed a somewhat less complex scheme which he labeled an index of imbalance.

> The net favorable/unfavorable score (the difference between a party's percentage of favorable and unfavorable "statements") for the Democrats was 6.5 unfavorable. The net favorable/unfavorable score for the G.O.P. was 14.9 favorable. The difference between the two scores (algebraic), termed the index of imbalance, was 21.4 favorable to the Republicans [51, p. 299].

Batlin's system, then, provides a quantified test, loosely equated with intensity, based solelv on frequency.

Rucker [202], in a study of wire service reports of crowds during the 1956 presidential campaign, employed an interesting technique for analyzing direction. He used a panel of thirty judges to classify 120 relevant items on an 11-point scale of favorableness (1 = least unfavorable, 6 = neutral, 11 = most favorable). The judgments of the panelists were statistically analyzed to develop indices for comparing coverage by wire services and for trend analyses. It should be noted, however, that the use of this system does not eliminate the requirement for composing a complete set of definitions outlining what is to be considered favorable and unfavorable content.

Another successful approach to analyzing direction lies in thematic analysis. While the theme is considered a unit of measurement in content analysis (see Chapter 6), it also may be among the more objective methods of determining direction. Berelson defines a theme as "an assertion about a subject matter. Thus, it is a sentence (or sentence-compound), usually a summary or an abstracted sentence, under which a wide range of specific formulations can be subsumed" [2, p. 138]. In content analysis the theme has also been referred to as an assertion, an idea unit, a proposition, and a variety of other labels.

What is the value of the theme in analysis of direction? The answer to this question is probably best shown by citing an example from Berelson. Suppose that in several editorials a number of assertions appeared claiming that in the United States "there are political and economic injustice, plutocratic exploitation, war profiteering, Communist sedition, Jewish conspiracy, and spiritual decay." All these assertions can be grouped under a central theme: The United States is internally corrupt. Any other assertions indicating internal corruption would also appear under this theme heading. Concerning the central theme itself, the analyst is not required to make a judgment—he is not required to label the central theme as being favorable or unfavorable toward the United States. At the same time, the central theme obviously does denote direction. Now, whereas the researcher can and should draw inferences from and comment liberally upon such direction, his findings do not reflect a high degree of subjectivity because he has merely counted and listed assertions, rather than defining idea units as favorable and others as favorable. The analyst must, of course, categorically list the elements in each main theme (sometimes called theme categories). And, naturally, each theme classified *must* be considered in the context in which it was used.

INTENSITY OF DIRECTION

Closely related to direction is *intensity,* and here we move into a difficult and oftentimes highly controversial area of content analysis. As has been pointed out, direction merely determines whether the content (or symbol) expresses an opinion or makes a statement that is for or against a given object, person, group, or activity. Intensity is the strength or degree of the conviction expressed. In simpler terms, do the content symbols mildly oppose or favor or do they vehemently oppose or favor a given object, person, group, or activity? In the strictest sense of the word, intensity probably refers to the strength and degree to which a given point of view is developed in *and through the symbols or combination of symbols of the manifest content.* This means, simply, that intensity refers to the strength of the language (the words) used to endorse or denounce a given object, person, group, or activity. In even broader terms, intensity discussed on this level refers to the intensity of the content symbols of a given assertion or single item of content.

However, intensity can be recognized in another sense, i.e., from a composite point of view. Whereas each individual item on, for example, a printed page may have a certain intensity level, the overall manner in which the material is presented constitutes another form of intensity. By scanning two or three publications, the reader may come to the conclusion that one publication has given a series of items considerably stronger emphasis than another publication—a factor which most certainly elicits some psychological reaction from the reader. In other words, the overall impact of presentation—including frequency, page placement, and headline size, among other things—is also a measure of intensity that must be taken into account. In the following paragraphs, examples of various methods used by different analysts to determine intensity in the two approaches will be discussed.

INTENSITY OF CONTENT SYMBOLS

Lasswell, Lerner, and Pool expressed their opinion about intensity as follows:

> Here the problem is to supplement frequency and amount by other criteria which can be applied metrically to symbolic behavior. Although the procedures available for measuring intensity require improvement, it is now possible . . . to reach some valid conclusions concerning intensity of attitudes expressed in symbols [24, p. 37].

Osgood feels that intensity of direction can be obtained through the analysis of connectors (verb phrases) and common-meaning evaluators (modifiers). He suggests assigning weights in terms of a seven-step scale running from −3 to +3, depending on the strength of the connector or evaluator used in conjunction with the object being described.

> In general, strong intensity (±3) is carried by the verb "to be" (X *is* a Y), the verb "to have" (X *does not have* Y), and most unqualified simple verbs when used in the present tense (X *loves* Y); moderate intensity (± 2) is carried by verbs implying imminent, partial, probably, increasing, etc., association or dissociation (X *plans to* or *is trying to do* Y), by tenses other than the present (X *has favored* Y), and by most modal auxiliary forms (X *used to help* Y); weak intensity (±1) is carried by connectors which imply only possible or hypothetical relation between actor and complement (X *may commit, might agree with, ought to join* Y). Indexing adverbs are also useful guides, for example, *absolutely, definitely, positively* (±3), *normally, ordinarily, usually* (±2), *slightly, occasionally,* and *somewhat* (±1) [31, p. 48].

Much the same approach is proposed to determine the intensity of evaluative common-meaning material:

> Although there are no formal rules for judging the intensity of evaluation, coders seem to have little difficulty if they keep in mind that the three degrees (3, 2, 1) should be used with roughly equal frequency over large samples of material. We have found that the linguistic quantifiers "extremely," "quite," and "slightly" provide roughly equal units here. Thus, *fair play* seems extremely favorable in our culture and *atrocities* extremely unfavorable; *sympathetic* seems quite favorable and *disturbing* quite unfavorable; *interesting* seems slightly favorable and *tense* slightly unfavorable. Again, the use of adverbs as modifiers of adjectives and adjectives as modifiers of nouns often provide helpful cues; for example, X was *extremely honest,* X was a *perfect gentleman* [31, p. 48].

Osgood's scheme for evaluative assertion analysis (developed more fully on page 62) gives an indication of the intensity of manifest content based solely on the language structure of a given culture. It measures the use of certain words that have a commonly accepted or modal-symbol strength in terms of a given culture. The implied assumption is that the communicator, recipient, and coder of the message being analyzed assign the same strength to certain connectors and evaluators.

IMPACT AS INTENSITY

A number of other devices have been developed to measure intensity of direction. Price [197] devised a scale based on reports of significant events, headline display, news-story content, and illustrations. On the basis of this scale, he drew the profile of each newspaper in the study to compare performance in each of the specified areas.

The attention-score device referred to in Chapter 5 allows comparison between the amount of space occupied and the type of emphasis given favorable and unfavorable news. The findings yielded by such measures can be loosely equated with intensity. Whereas raw data (such as the number of items placed in direction categories) show only the *frequency* of units of favorable and unfavorable material, the attention score indicates the relative emphasis given favorable and unfavorable material. For example, if we assume the unit of measurement is items and the raw data show that newspapers A and B each has five favorable and five unfavorable items, reference to the attention scores assigned the items on the basis of weight might indicate that news-A gave the favorable news preferential treatment whereas newspaper B emphasized the unfavorable news. To determine intensity through frequency from the statistical standpoint, you can examine the variance of percentages computed for the samples of various lengths (usually consisting of consecutive days). This should reveal intensity levels.

DETERMINING TRENDS

Establishing trends is not limited to consideration of direction, although trend analysis has been used most effectively in the area of direction analysis. A trend refers to the *increase* or *decrease* of the frequency of given symbols (or content) over a period of time. Normally, trend analysis is done after the basic quantification of the material has been completed. For example, assume an analyst is measuring and classifying material as either favorable or unfavorable toward a given object, person, or group over a three-month period. After his measurements are completed, he could isolate the favorable or unfavorable figures broken down by weeks. He can then note whether there is a relatively constant increase or decrease in the amounts of material presented over the three-month period.

Brown [284], in his study of anti-Catholic documents circulated during the 1960 presidential election campaign, constructed what he called a density level for the detection of trends. His basic unit of measurement was the assertion (a single thought unit). The assertion density level was a computed index that showed the mean number of assertions per 100 words in each document. By applying his index, Brown was able to determine whether or not there had been an increase in unfavorable material as the date of the national election drew nearer. Trend charts, such as the one adapted from Brown's study (Figure 5), show that certain content elements are clearly related to time. In this instance, the number of anti-Catholic assertions in a group of selected extremist publications increased sharply as the 1960 election day drew

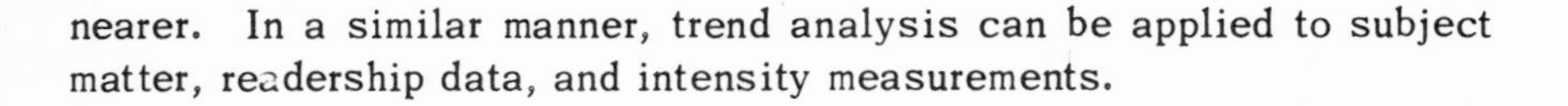

nearer. In a similar manner, trend analysis can be applied to subject matter, readership data, and intensity measurements.

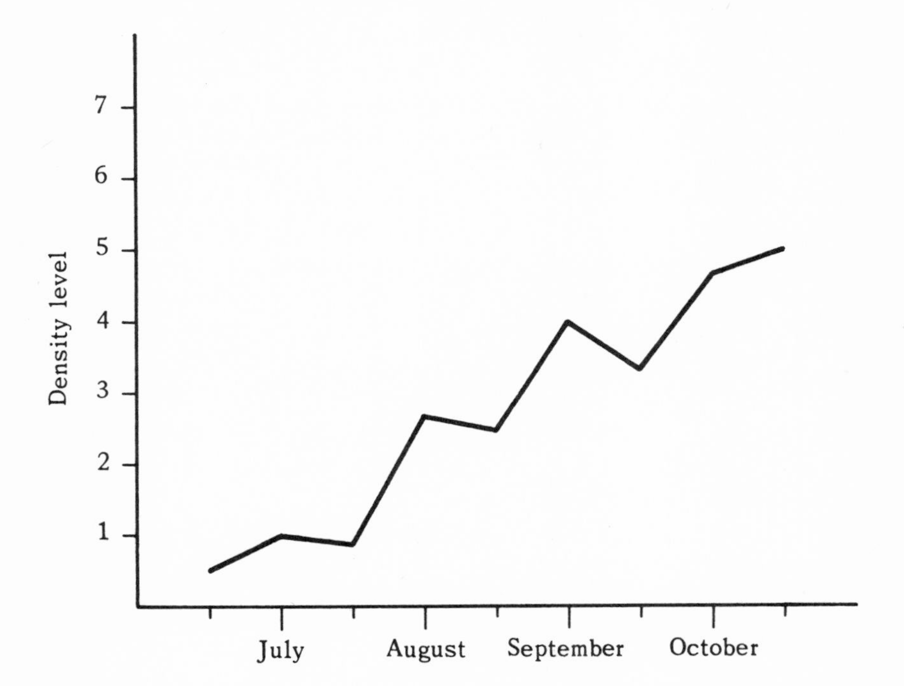

Figure 5/ The density level of anti-Catholic assertions in extremist publications during the 1960 presidential campaign. Density level is computed on the basis of assertions per 100 words. (Adapted from an unpublished study by Lee M. Brown [284].)

In another approach to the analysis of trend, Haskins suggests the use of the Spearman rank-order-correlation method. He points out that rank-order correlation gives a measure that is

> . . . expressed in a convenient numerical form which is sufficiently precise to compare with other such figures, takes into account all the data. . . . statistical significance can be determined by reference to a table, and the statistic is quickly computed. It is also easily interpreted, the limits being a perfectly consistent upward trend indicated by +1.00, a perfectly consistent downward trend by −1.00, and holding steady or no trend by zero. . . . In assigning ranks to the time period, rank one [1] should be assigned to the most recent time period [rank two (2) to the next most recent, etc.]; in assigning ranks to the other variable [direction data, subject-matter material, etc.], the largest figure gets rank one. In this way, the sign of the coefficient will correctly indicate the direction of the trend, a minus [−] coefficient for a declining trend and a plus [+] for a rising trend [127, p. 83].

But, as Haskins also points out, the rank-order-correlation method will not measure the magnitude of the trend.

> For example, a perfectly consistent increase from 10 to 15 in a time period would show the same perfect upward trend (+1.00) as a perfectly consistent increase from 10 to 100.
> Neither does the measure indicate the shape of the trend; an accelerating decrease (20, 19, 17, 14, 10), a decelerating decrease (20, 16, 13, 11, 10), or a constant-rate decrease (20, 18, 16, 14, 12) would be indicated by −1.00 or perfect downward trend [127, p. 83].

EVALUATIVE–ASSERTION ANALYSIS

According to C. E. Osgood [30], the chief developer of the technique, evaluative-assertion analysis, minimizes analyst bias, enables researchers to clearly see its operations and conclusions and to easily replicate them, and gives its findings in meaningful numbers. But evaluative-assertion analysis is a tedious process, laborious and time consuming, as Osgood also points out.

Three elements are necessary to carry out this type of analysis. To begin, the investigator isolates *attitude objects* (AO_1); that is, symbols about which there could be differences of opinion as to evaluative meaning (for example, Marx, newspaperman, marriage). Of course, the attitude objects should be related to the variables being investigated. *Common-meaning terms* (*cm*)—verbal symbols on which there is common agreement (good, bad, honesty, massacre)—are the second required element. These terms, which may also be attitude objects (AO_2), are coupled with the attitude objects previously chosen (AO_1) to form the assertion to be analyzed.

A more reliable method is to extract the relevant elements from the content and recast them into assertions for analysis. During this step, symbols (usually meaningless) are used to hide the identity of the attitude objects. For example, in a study of news magazines' coverage of political conventions, Westley and his associates [250] designated the three leading candidates of each party as attitude objects; they substituted the term (symbol) "the candidate" for each man's name. (Where attitude objects are not of one class, they may be masked with any symbols meaningless to coders.) Thus, in the Westley study, an assertion might read: "The candidate has high ambition." But *XY* could have been used as the symbol for that particular candidate wherever his name appeared in the content.

The third element in evaluative-assertion analysis is *verbal connectors (c)* – the links between attitude objects and common-meaning terms. In the example cited above, "has" serves as the verbal connector; any verb found in the content—hates, conceals, supports—may be used.

A simple accounting scheme [29] is used to record the assertions and the coders' judgments of connectors and common-meaning terms (see Table 3). The verbal connectors and common-meaning terms are given numerical values. Each is rated on a seven-point scale, +3 to −3.

Table 3

1	2	3	4	5	6	7
Source (or number)	AO_1	c	Value, column 3	*cm* or AO_2	Value, column 5	Product, 4 x 6

Each attitude object's evaluation score may be computed by dividing the total of its score in column 7 by its modular sum of column 3; or all the attitude objects in column 7 may be totaled and divided by the total modular sum of column 3, depending on the demands of the problem. Osgood suggests an evaluation chart to display attitude object's averages; ranging from +3 to −3, the chart quickly shows which *AO*s were favorably treated, and which unfavorably.

The Westley group [250] used a slightly different method, scoring the candidates on two dimensions, evaluative (good-bad) and activity-potency (dynamism). Each assertion was first assigned to one of the dimensions, then coded plus, minus, or plus-minus (for statements that might be judged favorable by some but unfavorable by others, e.g., "The candidate is young.") The Westley group's study was considerably simpler to execute using this method than it would have been if Osgood's procedures had been strictly followed. As the authors noted, they "focused on a limited range of stories . . . and a limited number of attitude objects." This reduced the amount of labor but still provided a senstitive test of bias in the reporting of national political conventions.

As Osgood noted, however, evaluative-assertion analysis provides evaluations only of the message, "not what the source may have really intended." For this reason, he added, "it might yield predictions as to the effects on receivers better than inferences as to intentions of sources."

SYMBOL ANALYSIS

Most symbol studies, notably those undertaken by Harold Lasswell and his associates, have focused on political content; these authors provide the major rationale for studies of political symbols.

> We can study key political symbols as a concise means of surveying world history. We can observe symbol sequences to test scientific hypotheses about the communications process. . . . We can study variations in style, though the symbol user may not be conscious of them [23, p. 29].

The symbol analyst wishes to detect or describe some attitude or attitudes; he chooses symbols that describe those attitudes and looks for them in his content. Coding usually involves directional analysis—that is, noting whether the symbol is given favorable or unfavorable treatment—and the symbols may also be studied over time to determine changes in attention and treatment given a particular symbol. Pool in *Symbols of Democracy,* for example, "noted an increasing concern with the notion of democracy."

> Today the judgments expressed about democracy are strongly favorable, irrespective of the practice in a given country. The word DEMOCRACY itself was approved all through the last half-century in the British, French, and American editorials. The word is now always approved in the Russian editorials, too, although in the early years of the Bolshevik regime it was more often condemned than approved [272, p. 67].

To conduct his investigation, the symbol analyst needs to compile a list of symbols. The list might be compiled from a sample of the content, from relevant documents, or from other writings, or it could be prepared by experts in the subject under study. The Pool study, for example, used a list of democracy-relevant symbols and searched the content of fifty years of newspapers in five countries to determine attention and treatment. Additions to the symbol list may be made during the course of the investigation; however, this could require restudy of content previously coded—or faith in the expertness and alertness of the coders.

Symbols may be divided into references to persons and groups (symbols of identification), indications of preferences and volitions (symbols demand), and assumptions of fact (symbols of expectation) [24]. These classes are usable for study of any group or institution; but the symbol analyst may develop classes more relevant to his purposes.

Having counted symbols, and perhaps even classified them, the analyst may transpose his figures into percentages to show the attention trend for each symbol. He may compute correlation coefficients to investigate relationships between symbols; he may scrutinize the data for clusters of symbols that could provide an index to some trait or attitude. However, construction of an index ideally begins with the design of the study and attention to which symbols might logically serve as indicators of the concept, trait, or value being investigated. In a study of international violence, for example, indicators might be war, weapons, front, or enemy [24].

Interpreting the results of symbol analysis requires the analyst to distinguish between his symbol and its idea-referent, as Lasswell pointed out.

> These two things (symbol and idea-referent), though obviously related, are not the same. Sometimes fluctuations in a word may index fluctuations in a given idea; sometimes not. The increase in the use of the symbol DISARMAMENT during the interbellum probably reflects an actual increase in *concern* with the problem, but it certainly does not reflect an increase in the *act* of disarming [24, p. 44].

It is possible, perhaps even desirable, for the symbol analyst to compare the fluctuations in the use of his symbols to events. Such comparisons may enable him to develop predictors—an index of international tensions, for example, to predict international crises. Such comparisons should also demonstrate the necessity for distinction between a symbol and the idea to which it refers.

8

problems of reliability and validity

In simplest terms, *reliability* means repeatability with consistency of results; and *validity*, actually measuring what the researcher says he is measuring (e.g., trends in international tension, values in magazine fiction). Problems of reliability and validity are not confined to any one phase of content analysis; they must be reckoned with at every step: design, sampling, counting, analyzing, interpreting. Errors may creep into the research at any stage. Every researcher should consider reliability and validity during the design of his study, for at this early stage he may devise his measuring scheme and tests of reliability and, perhaps, validity. (Demonstration of validity is often difficult; many researchers ignore the question of validity entirely.)

RELIABILITY

Reliability need not be difficult to establish. In measurement, it means simply that investigators using the same techniques on the same material will get substantially the same results. It is often referred to as "stability." In content analysis, reliability may be viewed as a communication problem: How well will other researchers recognize the referent from the investigator's descriptions or coding instructions? Simple counting—for example, the number of times a key word or symbol appears—presents no problems. Assigning direction to statements, detecting propaganda themes, judging the strength of words–these operations may present the investigator and his coders with a greater challenge.

Some of the standard tests of reliability, of course, are available to the content analyst. Test-retest, equivalent-forms, and split-halves are adaptable to content analysis. In the test-retest method, the same test is used twice on the same population; if the order of the scores of subjects does not change appreciably from one test to the next, reliability (stability) has been established. For the content analyst, the test-retest method requires more than one coder using the same instructions to classify the same material. Thus the method tests the clarity of instructions and definitions and the ability of coders to follow instructions and comprehend definitions. How much variation should be allowed among coders is discussed below.

The split-halves technique requires division of the content, separate coding of the two halves, and comparison of results. Assignment of content–issues of newspapers, documents, broadcast segments–should be random to minimize differences due to time factors, differences between sources, and other random errors.

As a variation of the equivalent-forms technique Stempel [222] suggests computing a correlation coefficient of the results of two coders who coded the same material. To correct for random errors likely in frequency tabulation, a contingency table should be constructed for each pair of coders and a chi-square test run to determine coder reliability. This procedure calls for an item-by-item comparison of coders' work rather than a comparison of total results. In essence there is little difference in what Stempel sees as the equivalent-forms method and what others consider an adaptation of test-retest. Stempel also developed a percentage-agreement score, by which each coder's score would be based on his agreement with the majority. An item-by-item chart would show how each coder coded. As in other reliability checks involving several coders, this is a test of the coder's ability to follow instructions and of the instructions themselves. If one coder is consistently out of line with the others, he must be reinstructed or eliminated; if several coders are in disagreement, instructions and definitions must be reexamined.

How high must the coder's percentage be to qualify his work as reliable? There is no level generally agreed upon. But forms of content analysis should not be summarily rejected if reliability seems low. Rather, they should be developed and refined if they seem worthwhile departures from established methods. Of course, in content analysis, as in measurement generally, reliability in one study should be compared with similar studies.

Aside from the three forms of reliability tests discussed, other tests have used common statistical methodology. Brown [284], for example, selected five of his fellow graduate students, gave them his instructions (he had written them for himself), and asked them to code passages from his sample of campaign hate literature. He compared their results with his coding of the same passages, using the chi-square one-sample test as described in Siegel [34]. Had Brown's problem involved ranking items – e.g., ranking several editorials by degree of antagonism toward a presidential candidate – he might have used the Friedman two-way analysis of variance by ranks (also explained in Siegel), which is a test of whether the rankings resulted from chance assignment.

Scott [208] developed an index of intercoder agreement to be used in nominal-scale coding. As he explained, "By chance, alone, one would expect better agreement on a two-category than on a five-category scale." His reliability test was designed to eliminate this kind of bias. As with a number of other reliability tests, some knowledge of statistics is necessary to understand the operation.

No knowledge of statistical methods is needed to understand the formula offered by Holsti [29] to determine the reliability of two coders.

$$R = \frac{2\,(C_{1,2})}{C_1 + C_2}$$

$C_{1,2}$ is the number of category assignments both coders agree on, and $C_1 + C_2$ is the total of category assignments made by both coders. The formula could be extended for *n* coders.

Goldsen and Kaplan [23] found that coders, after detailed instructions could reach 90 per cent agreement in assigning headlines to categories, even with classifications that were somewhat vague (strength, morality). The authors, in another section of the same essay, stated that a correlation of .75 was considered too low for satisfactory reliability (for their purposes).

The analyst must decide what level of agreement—that is, of reliability – is satisfactory *to him* and should state in his report how he carried out his reliability tests and what the results were. The tests should be made before the analysis of the results of coding and counting. Otherwise, the analysis may not only reflect error in the coding and measurement, but compound it. Finally, reliability sets a limit to validity; a specific measure can be no more valid than it is reliable.

VALIDITY

In trying to determine the validity of his research, the investigator is asking if his methods produced the desired information. He may also be asking how well his concepts or variables fit his measurements of them. The literature of psychological tests and measurements abounds in references to validation procedures, but in the literature of content analysis, little attention has been paid to the subject. This is a problem that does not seem to weigh heavily on the minds of content analysts, particularly the occasional analysts. Judging from the literature, *direct validity* (also called face and logical validity) is often assumed by the content analyst. This method of validation presumes that a measure self-evidently measures what it is supposed to if the categories are rigidly defined and the coding has a high degree of reliability. While the analyst should give some attention to the processes involved in logical validation, the method should not be relied on by itself.

Whoever is concerned with scientific inquiry, and not mere purposeless exercises, must give considerable attention to methods of validation. Perhaps analysts would concern themselves more with validity if they viewed their techniques as instruments or tests—measurements of attention, tests of adherence to the party line. As Janis pointed out, the mere counting of words or other symbols presents no problem in validation. "The analyst's operations involve simple perceptual discriminations: determining the presence or absence of a given physical configuration and counting the number which are present" [23, p. 59]. If the investigation went no further, there would be no validation problem. Validity is important only if the words or symbols enumerated are to be used in scientific explanations. (But if they are not, why count them?)

Validity may be assessed by one or more methods, among them jury, known-group, independent-criterion, and construct-validity. The content analyst may wish to concern himself with predictive validity, too, if the aim of his research is to establish which content variables indicate characteristics of source or medium, for example.

The jury method of validation is an extension of logical validation but is considered slightly superior. Here, experts are asked to judge relevant parts of the methodology—choice and definition of variables, for example, or measuring techniques.

A variant of the jury is the known-group method, which uses known attitudes and characteristics of a group rather than its expertness. In content analysis, a sample of newspaper editorials could be subjected to thematic analysis. The themes could be compared to themes taken from content known to be consistent with, or contradictory to, the variable under study (e.g., in Lasswell's studies, United States periodicals could be compared with Nazi and Soviet propaganda to assess adherence to the propaganda themes).

Validation by an independent criterion is considered difficult but not impossible. Its attempt seems worthwhile if the investigator is interested in refining his techniques and weighing one against the other. In content analysis, this form of validation could be accomplished by making an evaluative-assertion analysis and checking its prediction validity by relating content characteristics to writer characteristics. Then the same content could be subjected to an evaluative *Q* sorting, a much simpler technique, and the results correlated with those obtained by the evaluative-assertion analysis. If the two methods correlate highly, the simpler technique might be used in future analyses, or evaluative-assertion analysis could be used on a sample of the content and the results correlated with those obtained by *Q* sorting.

A variation of the independent-criterion method of validation is convergent validation, in which different methods are used to measure the same variable. For example, in a study of cultural values, the analyst might use symbol analysis and theme analysis. He might also make separate studies of magazine fiction and television programs or motion pictures, best-selling novels or newspapers. Here, both methods and media would differ, because each medium would require a different approach.

CONSTRUCT VALIDITY

When a researcher is interested in knowing whether his research procedures are measuring the variables or attributes he wants to measure, he is interested in *construct validity,* which, according to Kerlinger, "unites psychometric notions with scientific theoretical notions" [21, p. 448]. This implies that the investigator has given some attention to theories. He should have constructed hypotheses, too, for one means of assessing construct validity is the empirical testing of hypotheses.

Kerlinger suggests factor analysis—reducing several measures to a few—as a step in construct validity. While this technique appears to have been little used in content analysis, some of its applications are suggested in the work of Tannenbaum and Lynch [237] and Taylor [241]. Tannenbaum and Lynch used the semantic differential and factor analysis in an attempt to measure sensationalism, and Taylor employed factor analysis as one step in developing content categories for a study of mental health news.

Correlation of variables is another useful procedure, according to Kerlinger. It implies attention to theories: What variables should be positively (or negatively) correlated? Construct validity is also suggested in the notions of convergent and discriminant validity, which use correlation; correlation is the empirical check. The known-group method of validation, too, is related to construct validity; here again, attention to theory is implied. Problems of validity (and of inference, too) might be considered in light of Osgood's remarks concerning contingency analysis (see Chapter 9).

> The use of the contingency method is based upon a very general inference about relations between messages and those who exchange them; namely, that contingencies among events in messages are indicative of the association structure in the source and predictive of the association structure that may result in the receiver. . . . But under what conditions is this general inference likely to be valid? Certainly one cannot make valid inferences about the total association structure of a liberal newspaperman hired to write editorials for the *Chicago Tribune!* In part, at least, the issue here comes down to precisely what question is being asked of the data. . . . If we are dealing with spontaneous informal messages from a single, known source . . . , source is probably most defensible. When dealing with deliberately planned messages, particularly when the "source" is an institution, . . . it would probably be safer to speak of the "policy" of the source. . . . In other words, here as elsewhere it is necessary for the analyst to take into account the total context from which the message appears [31, p. 73].

Thus, the researcher must ask, as Osgood suggests, "What do I want from my data?" Having answered that question in as specific terms as possible, the analyst turns to his variables and their definitions and asks whether they and his techniques will suffice for his purposes. The questions here, then, are concerned with reliability of technique and validity of the goals of the study.

9

analysis

In previous chapters we have discussed means of identifying and measuring variables relevant to content analysis studies. Now we turn our attention to the establishment of theoretical systems, a more basic problem of research, to help explain those things that we have observed and measured.

This is what the communication investigator seeks to do when he undertakes, by a study of message content and other variables, to attempt to define the environment in which the message was produced. He may want to find out which elements in the environment are connected with what kinds of communication behavior; he may also want to learn about the relationships of these variables to one another. To accomplish this, he must try to measure both the communication and environmental variables and then analyze them in such a way that he can draw inferences meaningful to his problem from the results. His goal is to identify those variables that help account for communication behavior and to discard those that do not.

To study the environment in which message behaviors occur, the researcher has at his disposal perhaps thousands of tests and scales. He may use these to measure such variables as the personalities, attitudes, aptitudes, intelligence, and levels of achievement of the persons involved, or the demographic characteristics of the environment, to mention only a few. For example, Donohew [91] used Taylor's "cloze procedure" [240], a technique based on the concept of closure, to study comprehension of good news and bad news about a political candidate among politically active and politically inactive subjects. One use of this procedure in content analysis studies might be to determine the relationship between a population of gatekeepers' comprehension of a certain kind of information and the way in which this information is passed through the gate. Thus, in studying the wire editor as a key gatekeeper, we might ask: Is his comprehension of complex stories related to the subsequent content and display of these stories in his paper? Does he tend to leave out parts he does not understand? What characteristics of the wire editor such as education are related to his understanding and to his including specific content in the stories for which he is responsible?

Analysis of problems such as these is usually best carried out with statistical tools, such as tests of differences between means, correlation coefficients, or more complex procedures involving several variables. It will not be the purpose of this chapter to catalog *all* the statistical tests which could possibly be used in the design of content studies. The procedures discussed in the following pages seemed to us to be among the most relevant.

TESTS OF DIFFERENCES

Suppose that an investigator wants to know if there is a real difference between the scores of newspapers in one kind of environment and those of newspapers in another, or between the scores of two kinds of news handlers in different situations. What he asks of a statistical test in these circumstances is that it tell him the probability that the difference between the scores as great as that observed could have occurred by chance. He draws inferences from the results.

Let us consider the case of an investigator who wants to find out if there is a significant difference between newspaper coverage of the war on poverty within poverty areas and outside poverty areas. Specifically, he wants to answer two main questions: Do newspapers in poverty areas run more stories on the issue than those in non-poverty areas? Do they run more stories classified as favorable? To answer these questions, the investigator may use any of a number of tests of differences. The choice of which to use depends in part on his sample size and in part on the nature of the data to be analyzed. Some tests that provide information about differences among groups are analysis-of-variance, chi-square test, t test, and Mann-Whitney U test, to name a few. The last mentioned test is most often used for samples of from nine to twenty.

The investigator may not wish to stop at one independent variable in looking for differences. He may wish to ask not only if newspapers in poverty areas give significantly different coverage from those in non-poverty areas, but also if large papers in poverty areas give different coverage from large ones in non-poverty areas and if the same is true of small papers. Or he may wish to subdivide his sample according to the newspapers' political affiliations or other variables. Here, a multivariate procedure, such as multivariate analysis of variance, might be appropriate.

CORRELATION

LINEAR

Suppose in your analysis of the general content of two daily newspapers, you wish to find out how alike they are in the emphasis they place on various categories of news. You could simply make a list for each paper, placing the category given the most space at the top of each list, the one with the next largest amount of space second, and so on, and make some judgments about the similarities or dissimilarities in the two lists. Or, you could take another step and statistically compute the relationship between the two publications.

Linear correlation is a statistical tool for determining the degree and direction of relationship between any two variables (or among several variables in multiple correlation), and is expressed as the *correlation coefficient* (r). Correlation can operate in two directions—negative and positive. The coefficient r ranges from a -1.0 (a perfect inverse or *negative* correlation), through 0.0 (the absence of any relationship), to +1.0 (a perfect *positive* correlation). For example, the correlation between height and weight generally produces a high positive coefficient, whereas the relationship between age and years of schooling for adults produces a negative correlation coefficient.

The graphs (scatter plots) in Figure 6 show patterns of relationship of varying magnitudes and the correlation coefficient for each. Assume A and B to be two newspapers and the plots to represent the averaged directional scores ranging from a -4 to a $+4$, for various categories of news. Each entry in each plot is fixed by the score for both papers in the same category. The first graph shows a high positive relationship ($r = .9$) between A and B; that is, paper A and paper B were pretty much alike in direction. For the most part, a category coded as high favorable (+) in paper A was coded as high favorable in paper B, thus keeping the scatter plot rather tight and the pattern quite definite.

On the second graph ($r = .4$), the scatter plot is more open. Although several categories were assigned the same scores in both papers, several were not, thus lowering the correlation between the two papers. The third plot ($r = 0.0$) reflects the absence of any relationship between the two publications. The last three plots indicate a negative correlation between the two newspapers. This is best seen in the last scatter plot

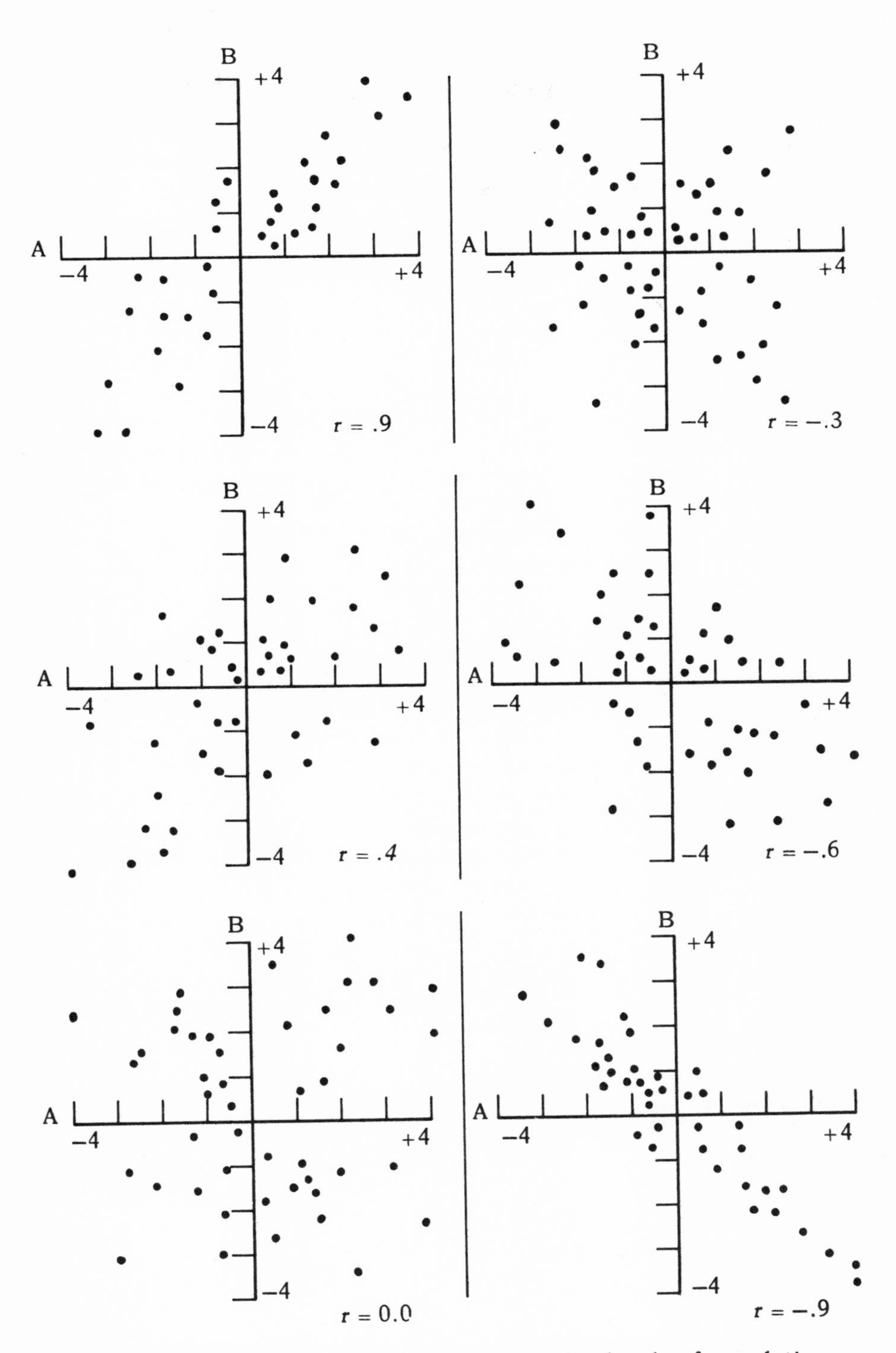

Figure 6/ Scatter plots of two variables at varying levels of correlation.

($r = -.9$), where the categories assigned high positive scores in paper B received the highest negative scores in paper A, and vice versa. Such a negative correlation might well be found in two antagonistic newspapers of differing political philosophy, for example.

There are a number of indices of linear correlation available. The Spearman rank-order and Kendall rank-order indices of correlation are nonparametric. These coefficients are easily computed by ranking the data in lists as suggested earlier. You will recall Haskins' use of the Spearman method for determining trends outlined in Chapter 7. The Pearson product-moment method is considered to be more precise than the rank-order methods, because it is computed on the basis of the actual scores involved rather than simple rank-order. As with tests of differences, the choice of procedures should depend partly on the size of the sample and partly on the nature of the measurements made on the two variables.

If the investigator were studying not only the relationship of attitude to content scores but also the relationship of other variables to content, he might use one of the multivariate procedures. These include multiple correlation and multiple regression, partial correlation, canonical correlation, and factor analysis. This section is not intended to provide instruction in statistics, but rather to acquaint the investigator with possible uses of a few of the better known and more useful procedures.

MULTIPLE CORRELATION AND REGRESSION

Although simple correlation procedures are useful in that they allow us to examine individual relationships between variables, the investigator seeking to make predictions will find that very rarely do two variables provide him with enough information. For example, he may find that the simple (zero-order) correlation between content direction and publisher attitude is .60, thus accounting for 36 per cent ($.60^2 \times 100$) of the variance of content. Repeating his correlation procedure, he may find that content direction is also correlated with circulation at .60; thus circulation also accounts for 36 per cent of the variance. What the investigator cannot learn from this procedure is whether the second variable has accounted for additional variation, giving him up to 72 per cent of the content variation accounted for, or whether the two variables overlap each other entirely, leaving him with only 36 per cent of the variation accounted for and thus not improving his ability to predict variation in content. What is needed here is a procedure that will let him know how much predictively useful information he has gained with each new independent variable he adds.

Such a procedure is multiple correlation and regression, which involves analysis of the relationship between one dependent variable, such as news coverage, and two or more independent (predictor) variables. The main aim of this procedure is to provide an equation for making predictions. As Borko [3] has noted, the multiple-regression model has been used primarily with very small groups of variables for the purpose of obtaining weights that, when applied to predictors, would yield optimal predictions of observed criteria. Thus an investigator may learn, following multiple-regression analysis involving several variables, that he can make fairly reliable predictions about the degree of favorableness of newspaper coverage on a given issue by finding out only two things about the population of newspapers he wants to investigate. For example, he may find that he can successfully predict the kind of coverage if he knows the attitude of the publisher and the circulation of the paper. Perhaps the major dividend from his analysis through multiple correlation and multiple regression is a prediction equation — a formula for predicting coverage once he has the other information.

PARTIAL

The investigator may wish to go beyond determining what combination of independent variables, such as publisher attitude and circulation, contribute most to predicting how things will turn out. He may also want to know the independent effects of these variables as predictors. One way of learning this is through a partial-correlation procedure, in which the effect of each predictor variable is studied separately, with the effects of other predictors removed.

CANONICAL

Canonical correlation somewhat resembles multiple correlation except that whereas multiple correlation describes the relationship of two or more independent variables to a single dependent variable, canonical correlation is used when there is also more than one dependent variable. This procedure makes it possible to determine the maximum correlation between a *set* of predictor variables and a *set* of criterion variables. For example, let us consider the same situation as above, in which publisher attitude and size of newspaper are the independent (predictor) variables. However, instead of using only scores on favorableness of the content as the single measure of coverage, let us assume we have two measures: content favorableness scores and display scores. (Methods for calculating such scores through content analysis procedures are described in the sections on directional analysis and the display index.) Therefore, we want to know the maximum relationship of two things – publisher attitude and newspaper size – taken together, to two more things – content scores and display scores – also considered together. As in the multiple correlation-multiple regression situation, one result of the analysis is an equation – involving weights for all variables, predictors, and criteria – for predicting the coverage from the independent variables.

CONTINGENCY ANALYSIS

Contingency analysis is a method of testing the association structure in a message source (what ideas are related in the source's thinking) by the content contingencies (the co-occurrence of symbols). Its application is somewhat limited in regard to messages in the mass media, for the investigator usually will not have detailed data on the person who produced the message. It is also limited, as Osgood, its innovator, pointed out, in that an analyst "cannot make valid inferences about the total association structure of a liberal newspaperman hired to write editorials for the *Chicago Tribune*" [31, p. 73]. However, contingency analysis could be a useful procedure for analyzing propaganda, signed editorials or columns (where the writer's freedom had been ascertained), or letters to the editor.

Two major choices must be made by the investigator using contingency analysis – the unit of content and categories. Some content falls into natural units – paragraph, editorial, column, letter. However, if the unit is too small, contingencies (co-occurrence) will probably be fewer. Categories may be chosen by noting which relevant subjects (or symbols) – democracy, youth, Communists – are most often used by the source. Or they may be clearly specified by the focus of the research problem. The investigator should avoid almost-synonymous categories, of course, as he should avoid too-inclusive categories that actually include unlike symbols.

Having chosen units and categories, the analyst reads the content, noting the presence or absence of each category in each unit. Osgood suggests a raw-data matrix, with the units serving as rows and the categories as columns. If a content category is present, a plus sign is recorded in the appropriate row and column; recording a minus sign indicates the absence of reference to a specific category in a specific unit. The frequency of any category in any one unit is not important; for example, if "democracy" is mentioned three times in one paragraph (the unit), it is recorded as a single plus, not as three.

From the raw-data matrix, a contingency matrix is constructed, using categories for both rows and columns. The upper-right cells contain the expected (chance) frequencies; the lower-left cells, the obtained or actual contingencies (the percentage of units in which plusses appear in both columns being tested). If the obtained figure is greater than the expected value, the events are co-occurring more often than they would be by mere chance. The significance of the difference between the obtained and expected values can be tested by chi square (which Osgood feels is too laborious) or by the simple standard error of the percentage used by Osgood.

Another form of analysis is to inspect the contingency matrix and note the categories that are related in the same way, e.g., always positively or always negatively. These clusters can be isolated and presented graphically to show the message source's association structure.

FACTOR ANALYSIS

Referring to the example used in discussing linear correlation (a comparison of the directional scores of two newspapers for various categories), assume that instead of directional scores, you have a set of attention scores for each news category, and that instead of two, you have twenty newspapers. There would, of course, be no mechanical problem in developing a complete set of intercorrelations (a correlation matrix); correlation coefficients would be developed between each paper and every other paper in the group. Paper A would be correlated with paper B, paper A with paper C, . . . , paper B with paper C, paper B with paper D, and so on, until all the correlation coefficients (190) had been developed. You can see that this would present quite a problem in interpretation and would certainly create a complex job of describing just exactly what had been found.

What is needed in this case is some method of analyzing and synthesizing or boiling down these interrelationships into meaningful patterns – and doing so without sacrificing important information. With the data in matrix form (see Table 4), you can see, by inspecting the correlations, that several papers are highly correlated to each other, while showing much less relationship to others. By submitting the correlations to *factor-analysis* procedures, you can determine which papers group together in terms of similar content emphasis.

The basis of factor analysis is linear correlation. The first step in any factor-analysis program, then, is the development of a correlation matrix. To better describe how factor analysis works, and how – at least in one instance – it was applied to content analysis, we shall examine a study conducted by the late Paul J. Deutschmann [11] in which he analyzed the news content of several metropolitan daily newspapers. For the example, the discussion will be confined to that part of the study that centers on the seven New York City daily newspapers.*

Deutschmann developed what he called an emphasis score for each of forty-nine content categories. In essence, these scores showed the relative emphasis placed on the various categories of news. Each paper was correlated with every other paper on the basis of the scores to develop the matrix in Table 4.

Table 4/ Matrix of Correlations between Papers by Full Set of Category Emphasis Scores

Newspaper	T	HT	W-T&S	P	J-A	N	M
Times	----	.86	.52	.41	.38	.39	.28
Herald Tribune	.86	----	.81	.67	.73	.66	.57
World-Telegram & Sun	.52	.81	----	.83	.88	.72	.73
Post	.41	.67	.83	----	.92	.68	.74
Journal-American	.38	.73	.88	.92	----	.64	.69
News	.39	.66	.72	.68	.64	----	.93
Mirror	.28	.57	.73	.74	.69	.93	----

LINKAGE ANALYSIS

Even a matrix of the size shown in Table 4 presents some problems in analysis and description. Inspecting the coefficients visually can be of some help, but a procedure developed by McQuitty [176] known as linkage analysis describes the data a little more succinctly and, at the same time, helps to explain factor analysis. In linkage analysis, clusters are developed on the basis of groupings of high intercorrelations. For example, the *New York Times* had its highest correlation with the New York *Herald Tribune* (r = .86), and the *Herald Tribune* was correlated most highly with the *Times* (r = .86). Since none of the other five newspapers had their highest correlation with either the *Herald Tribune* or the *Times*, these two papers formed a cluster of their own. Following the same procedure for the remaining publications, you can develop the linkage pattern shown in the accompanying illustration. The linkage analysis shows, quite clearly, three clusters of newspapers, as described by Deutschmann:

A. A tabloid couplet — the *NY News* and the *NY Mirror* are very similar in their play of the news, and they are least like the *NY Times*.

*Deutschmann's study, "News-page Content of Twelve Metropolitan Dailies," was conducted in 1959 and included the New York City daily newspapers, which at that time were seven in number. In the years since the time of the study, the *New York Mirror* discontinued publication, and the *New York Herald Tribune, New York World-Telegram & Sun,* and *New York Journal-American* merged; the new paper is called the *World Journal Tribune*. Deutschmann's data are used here in their original form to demonstrate how factor analysis could be used to extend them.

B. A standard trio — The *Journal-American* and *Post* are the central papers in this group, which also includes the *World-Telegram-Sun*.

C. A quality couplet – The *New York Times* and *Herald Tribune* [11, p. 95].

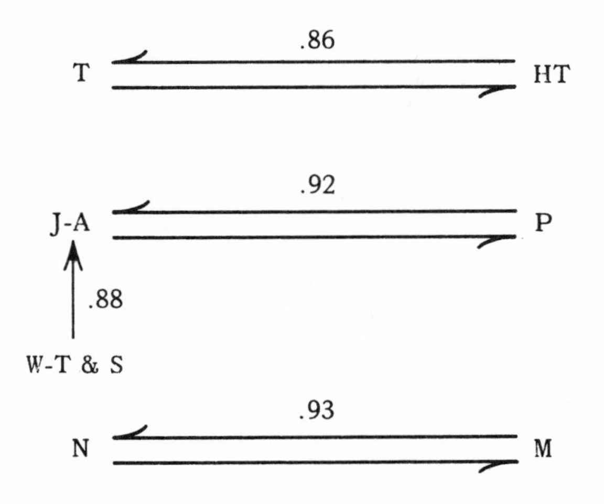

On the surface, this grouping of the seven newspapers appears to make sense. It is probably the kind of grouping, on the basis of content, that most of us would make.

While the linkage analysis does help in synthesizing the data, it only skims the available information. For example, further inspection of the correlation matrix shows that while the *Herald Tribune* had its highest correlation with the *Times* ($r = .86$), it also had a fairly high correlation with the *World-Telegram & Sun* ($r = .81$) and moderately high correlations with the other four papers. In other words, the three factors are not what is called pure. While the linkage-analysis diagram might appear tidy and logical, the matrix shows that the solution of the problem is not quite so simple. At least one or more of the newspapers appearing to be in one of the groups may also have some variance in common with another group. To help answer these and other questions about the data, one needs a method more thorough than the inspection method. Here, factor analysis will be used.

CENTROID METHOD

Continuing to use Deutschmann's data as the example, we submitted the correlation matrix to centroid factor analysis rotated to Thurstone simple structure. A computer program was available for this method of analysis, thus reducing immensely the amount of labor required to do it. Many other methods of factor analysis and factor rotation, such as principle axis and varimax, are available.

Table 5/ Factor Matrix of Data from Emphasis Correlation Matrix (Rotated Solution)

Newspaper	Oblique factors	
	I	II
Times	.768	.000
Herald Tribune	.630	.349
World-Telegram & Sun	.167	.694
Journal-American	.002	.790
Post	−.009	.786
News	.007	.739
Mirror	−.159	.853

The roman numerals I and II in Table 5 refer to the factors found in the analysis. This is a two-factor solution, meaning that the seven newspapers fell into two groups rather than the three that the linkage analysis showed. The entries in the matrix are referred to as *factor loadings,* which have the same range as do correlation coefficients, from −1.0 (maximum negative) through 0.0 (indicating no relationship) to +1.0 (maximum positive). To describe the findings, one would say that .768 is the factor loading for the *Times* on factor I, .853 is the factor loading for the *Mirror* on factor II, and the *Herald Tribune* had a loading of .630 on factor I and .349 on factor II.

The analysis shows that the content emphasis of the *Times* and the *Herald Tribune* constituted one factor, and the other five papers made up the second factor in terms of emphasis on categories of content. Also, the *Mirror* loaded negatively (−.159) on factor I and had the highest loading (.853) on factor II.

The statistical analysis, however, is not the end of the investigation. To find out what elements make the *Times* and the *Herald Tribune* more like each other and different from the other papers, it is necessary to return to the original data. It would also be interesting to find out why the *Mirror* and the *News,* which intuitively and through linkage analysis might have been thought to be a separate group, appeared in the factor analysis to be grouped with the other three "standard" newspapers. However, it is readily seen that factor analysis has provided the synthesis and economy originally desired and has pointed up the dangers inherent in visual inspection and interpretation of data. Considering the superabundance of data with which the content analyst usually has to cope, there will probably be continued development and application of summarizing techniques like factor analysis.

OTHER APPROACHES

There are several ways of correlating and factoring the data derived from content analyses. Raymond Cattell [68] describes a number of such schemes, and their relevance for communication research is discussed by MacLean [168]. We include a summary of MacLean's discussion here because the impact of using these techniques in content analysis could be most significant.

The traditional factor analysis is developed from what is known as *R analysis,* which is the correlating and factoring of tests for a sample of persons – or, another example, categories for a sample of newspapers – holding time constant. The *R* matrices developed would take the following form (adapted from MacLean's presentation):

R Score Matrix

	News categories						
Newspapers	1	2	3	.	.	.	*k*
A	4	2	8	.	.	.	4
B	6	4	10	.	.	.	2
C	10	8	10	.	.	.	8
.	.	.	.	.	.	.	.
.	.	.	.	.	.	.	.
.	.	.	.	.	.	.	.
n	4	10	6	.	.	.	4

Assuming that the entries in the score matrix represent attention scores assigned to the various categories, it can be seen that newspaper A gave low attention to category 2, newspaper B gave high attention to category 3, and so on. The next step in *R* analysis is to correlate category 1 with category 2, category 1 with category 3, and so on, forming the *R* correlation matrix.

R Correlation Matrix

	News categories						
News categories	1	2	3	.	.	.	*k*
1	---	–.02	.15	.	.	.	.42
2	–.02	---	.29	.	.	.	.07
3	.15	.29	---	.	.	.	.19
.	.	.	.	.	.	.	.
.	.	.	.	.	.	.	.
.	.	.	.	.	.	.	.
k	.42	.07	.19	.	.	.	---

Here, we see that category 1 correlated .42 with category *k* and that category 2 correlated .29 with category 3. The correlation .42 indicates a tendency for newspapers that emphasize category 1 also to emphasize category *k*; and for those that deemphasize category 1 also to deemphasize category *k*. The next step is the factor analysis that generates a matrix in the form shown below.

R Factor Matrix

	Factors				
News categories	I	II	III	IV	V
1	.68	.16	.06	–.05	.11
2	.03	.49	.23	.15	.15
3	.05	.54	.01	.21	.
.	.	.	.	.	.
.	.	.	.	.	.
.	.	.	.	.	.
k	.59	–.05	.15	.10	.01

The matrix is read as before; e.g., categories 1 and *k* load high on factor I and have insignificant loadings on the other factors.

Now those items or categories that load high on the same factor can be examined for common characteristics. Such an approach could lead to collapsing certain content categories or developing new categories that reflect certain common patterns for subsequent analysis.

In Cattell's scheme, *Q analysis* is the inverse of *R*; that is, *Q* analysis correlates and factors persons for a sample of tests – or newspapers for a sample of items or scores. The Deutschmann analysis presented earlier is an example of this method. (Please note that we are referring to Cattell's *Q* analysis, not William Stephenson's *Q* methodology [37], which also involves the factoring of persons but is a considerably more complex concept than Cattell's.)

The result of a *Q* factor analysis (the correlation and factoring of persons or institutions or systems) is clusters of persons (or perhaps newspapers) showing similar patterns of interest (or attention or political view). The advantage of *Q*, as can be seen in the Deutschmann study, is that it may tell more about institutions or systems, or as MacLean puts it "anything of a symbolic nature which might elicit responses of theoretical interest to us, anything which identifies some characteristic of the 'person' " [168, p. 614]. Media institutions, it seems to us, quite decidedly qualify as a "person" role. You will remember that in the Deutschmann study, newspapers were the persons and the category emphasis scores were the tests. Deutschmann's correlation matrix was computed on the basis of rank-order correlations, each newspaper with every other newspaper. The factor analysis of this matrix discussed earlier was, then, a *Q* factor analysis.

The MacLean presentation [168] goes on to suggest the use of other schemes of Cattell.

P factor analysis, factors tests on a sample of the number of times they occur (or items or categories on a sample of times). MacLean suggests here that *P* might be used "in the historical study of a person, a community, a nation, a magazine, a television network, a newspaper."

O factor analysis, the reverse of *P*, factors across time on a sample of tests (or on a sample of items). The *O* analysis then factors occasions, situations. MacLean suggests here the possibility of studying changes in category emphasis throughout a newspaper's history.

T factor analysis factors across time for a sample of persons (or institutions). Here, the factor analysis shows us how occurrences cluster together in the way the institutions are ordered. An analyst might measure the amount of space devoted to military news by a sample of newspapers at various times – perhaps over a period of several years. The factor analysis would show which time periods go together; then the analyst could examine the time periods to find out what they had in common that might produce similar patterns of content in newspapers.

S factor analysis, the reverse of *T*, correlates and factors "persons" across time. This could show which media institutions tend to be alike in terms of how they respond to situations or occasions. An analyst might, for example, select time periods just prior to armed conflicts in which the United States has been involved. For S analysis, he would produce a matrix with the names of the media institutions across the top and the selected time periods down the side. The scores in the matrix would represent emphasis or direction scores of the content at that time.

Using the six analytic approaches suggested by Cattell, it is possible to come up with many more applications that might help clarify the basic data derived from a content analysis. To a great extent, the usefulness of content analysis will continue to grow with the imaginative application of some of the newer techniques of analysis, now made feasible with the high-speed electronic computer.

GUTTMAN'S RADEX

Another method of analyzing the data from the Deutschmann study can be drawn from the radex theory, developed by Louis Guttman [17] as a new approach to factor analysis. According to Guttman, the centroid method with rotation is based on the notion of common factors, while the radex theory is based on the notion of order factors.

> A set of variables whose intercorrelations conform to the general order pattern prescribed by the new theory will be called a *radex*. This word is designed to indicate a "radical expansion of complexity."
>
> Two distinct notions are involved in a radex. One is that of a difference in *kind* between tests, and the other is that of a difference in *degree*. Each of these notions will give rise to a separate concept of order among tests, so that the radex is ultimately at least a doubly ordered system [17, p. 260].

When variables differ from each other in the degree of their complexity (such as addition, subtraction, multiplication, and division), Guttman calls such a set of variables a *simplex*.

> It possesses a simple order of complexity. The tests can be arranged in simple rank order from least complex to most complex [17, p. 260].

On the other hand, where tests or variables have the same degree of complexity, they may differ among themselves only in the kind of ability they define.

> We shall postulate a law of order here too, but one which is not from "least" to "most" in any sense. It is an order which has no beginning and no end, namely, a circular order. A set of variables obeying such a law will be called a *circumplex,* to designate a "circular order of complexity" [17, p. 260].

Guttman states that tests can differ among themselves both in degree and in kind of complexity at the same time; this general structure is referred to as the radex.

> Thus, within a radex, one can usually isolate simplexes by keeping the content of the abilities constant and by varying the degree of complexity; and one can also usually isolate circumplexes by keeping degree of complexity constant and then varying content [17, p. 261].

THE SIMPLEX

Our use of Guttman's theory will be limited to a discussion of the simplex, although it seems to us that the whole of Guttman's radex can have general application to content analysis studies. The simplex stresses the notion of hierarchy and is based on the premise that one can attach meaning to a rank order among quantitative variables. Essentially, it is a single factor in which variables have been ordered on the basis of complexity.

The perfect simplex is formed where the observed intercorrelations between variables can be arranged in a matrix that is symmetric – where the correlations taper off or the gradient goes downward as you move down to the lower left of the matrix or upward toward the upper right of the matrix, with the largest correlations being adjacent to the main diagonal of the table. An example of a perfect simplex is reproduced in Table 6. If the variables in Table 6 had been equally spaced, there would have been a symmetrical curvilinear relationship between the rank of the column totals and the order of the variables. Since the variables were not equally spaced, this exact relationship did not occur.

In the factor matrix developed from Deutschmann's emphasis scores (Table 7), we noticed a strong hierarchical pattern, running from the *New York Times* downward to the *New York Mirror.* This suggested to us the possibility that Deutschmann's data might conform to Guttman's simplex model. Inspection of the original correlation matrix indicated

Table 6/ Test Intercorrelations for a Hypothetical Non-equally-spaced Perfect Simplex

Variable	v_1	v_2	v_3	v_4	v_5
v_1	1.00	.91	.63	.34	.11
v_2	.91	1.00	.72	.40	.19
v_3	.63	.72	1.00	.51	.44
v_4	.34	.40	.51	1.00	.87
v_5	.11	.19	.44	.87	1.00
Total	1.99	3.22	3.30	3.22	2.61

that with very little reorganization – using, as Guttman suggests, column totals for each variable's correlation coefficients to get started – we might be able to approach a simplex.

The matrix does confirm the fact that some hierarchy exists among the seven newspapers. We note the general trend for the largest correlations to be along the main diagonal and the tapering off of the coefficients to the lower-left and upper-right corners. But the data do not form a perfect simplex. The correlations between the *Journal-American* and the *News* and between the *World-Telegram & Sun* and the *Mirror* disrupt the pattern required of a perfect simplex. Guttman would call this matrix a *quasi-simplex*, because while the data do not form a perfect scale, they show definite gradients that indicate that some rank order of significance does exist.

While Guttman has developed mathematical definitions of the quasi-simplex, we shall not go into them at this point. Guttman would, in any event, suggest that the next step be an inspection of the ordering to see if it makes any sense. Because of the simplex form, we are now looking at the seven newspapers on a more-or-less single plane, ordered by complexity (in this case complexity of emphasis). Our interpretation would say that we range from the *New York Times* as most complex to the *New York Mirror* as the least complex; that the *Times* is more complex than any of the others; that the *Herald Tribune* is less complex

Table 7/ Reorganization of Intercorrelations Between Papers by Full Set of Category Emphasis Scores

Newspaper	T	HT	WT&S	J-A	P	N	M
Times	----	.86	.52	.38	.41	.39	.28
Herald Tribune	.86	----	.81	.73	.67	.66	.57
World-Telegram & Sun	.52	.81	----	.88	.83	.72	.73
Journal-American	.38	.73	.88	----	.92	.64	.69
Post	.41	.67	.83	.92	----	.68	.74
News	.39	.66	.72	.64	.68	----	.93
Mirror	.28	.57	.73	.69	.74	.93	----
Total	2.84	4.30	4.49	4.24	4.25	4.02	3.94

than the *Times*, but more complex than any of the remaining five; and so on. The ordering appears to make sense.

FACET ANALYSIS

Although facet analysis (also termed dimension analysis) has not been widely applied to problems of content analysis, it is applicable; and some pioneer studies have indicated its value. Sometimes called "the poor man's factor analysis," facet analysis was developed by Louis Guttman [115, 116] from mathematical set theory. Guttman's facets more closely resemble Fisher's factors than they do the factors of Thurstone and Spearman. Facet analysis makes use of what is known as the *contiguity metahypothesis:* Things (variables) close together semantically will be close together statistically.

There are two approaches to facet analysis; one is to start with a correlation matrix. In content analysis, this matrix could be constructed from the frequency distribution of the variables, and the metahypothesis is restated: Things close together statistically will be close together semantically. The correlation matrix is examined for strong positive or negative relationships; pairs positively related should be closer together semantically than pairs negatively related. Both positive and negative correlations may help the analyst trace the patterns and provide a means of exploring the "why" of content characteristics. Or the positive pairs may indicate that some combining of categories is possible; each pair may be two elements of one facet. Negative correlations may also indicate facets, with each variable being an element of the facet or dimension (e.g., an intellectualism-unreflective dimension).

The other approach to facet analysis is to conceive the research problem in terms of its facets or dimensions and to diagram all relationships possible in a set of *n* facets with *k* elements. Using the contiguity metahypothesis, some of the probable statistical relationships could be hypothesized and examined through the empirical research.

Facet analysis may be introduced at any of several stages of a research problem. Harrison and MacLean [264], for example, isolated the three facets of facial expression – eyebrows, eyes, and mouth – and designed their research to get at the responses to the various combinations of the facets. They used factor analysis of responses and faces; then, using a scheme from Guttman's facet theory, they constructed four levels of expression and suggested chains in expression change.

MacLean has suggested another use of facet analysis, "to determine what picture elements (in newspaper and magazine photographs) relate most closely to reader responses of excitement, stimulation, interest." He based the design on previous research.

> . . . we developed a dimension or facet, A, for facial expression with three elements or levels: a_1 violent expression, contorted face, a_2 moderate expression such as smile or frown and a_3 no expression or no person. And we have a second facet, B, for movement of person or object, with three levels similar to those above.
>
> The fame or importance of a person or thing pictured seemed to be another facet. . . . We split this C facet simply into two levels. Then, we constructed a fourth facet to deal with broad categories which seem to define different areas of interest: d_1 fine arts, sculpture, . . . , d_2 science and technology, d_3 social, business, political, etc. and d_4 sports and entertainment [268, p. 19].

From this four-facet design with twelve elements, seventy-two combinations of elements were possible (3 x 3 x 2 x 4 = 72). In order to conduct the analysis of responses to content, it was necessary to find photographs for each of the seventy-two kinds of content. The contiguity-metahypotehsis was applied in the following way.

> . . . if we have two pieces of complex content which differ from each other in only one semantic element, responses to them should be associated more closely statistically than those to two pieces which differ from each other in several semantic elements. In other words, $a_1b_1c_1d_3$ and $a_1b_2c_1d_3$ should correlate more closely than either does with $a_3b_3c_2d_1$ [268, p. 20].

Approaching a content analysis problem through facet analysis (facets and their elements) may be valuable in suggesting new ways of looking at the problem or at the data already extracted from the content. One advantage is that facet analysis includes a facet model, an analog to the Guttman scale, that shows how and why it should result in a simplex correlation matrix. (For Guttman's facet model, see [116]).

USING STATISTICS

As we stated earlier, no attempt has been made to provide a complete inventory of statistical procedures appropriate to content studies. In presenting these procedures of analysis discussed in this chapter, it was our intent to provide a brief outline of each and to suggest some possible applications.

The authors would like to stress that statistical tools are not to be used like aspirin—mere application is not a cure for research headaches. Legitimate employment of any statistical test requires that certain assumptions be met concerning the population under study, the sample employed, the manner in which observations are derived, the measurement techniques involved, and so on. It is true that the assumptions required for nonparametric statistical tests are less stringent than those attending the use of parametric tests, but they are present.

In essence, we wish to issue a word of advice: If you are going to undertake a study in which you will be using statistical tests, you should first learn something about statistics and what it is you can accomplish by employing such methods. The rationale, the statistical requirements, and the formulas for tests applicable to content analysis that are included in this text and others can be found in many of the several books listed in the bibliography.

10

content analysis and the computer

The computer, as an instrument of organization and analysis, has become a basic research tool in all areas of behavioral science. As researchers learn more and more about human behavior (and content analysis is merely a means of investigating another form of human behavior), they become increasingly aware that the problems of studying man as he interacts with his society and his environment are infinitely more complex than was assumed. Because of this knowledge the researcher's approach to learning more about human behavior necessarily becomes more complex in design. It is the particular ability of the computer to solve complex problems – at incredibly high speeds – that has made it so valuable, and will continue to increase its value, to the social scientist. Dr. Harold Borko writes:

> In the growth of computer technology, man is assigning increasingly complex tasks to the machine and, in turn, is freeing himself to assume increasingly more complex tasks. From subjects as basic as perception, learning, and thinking, through analysis of specialized social organizations [which would include the mass media of communication] man is harnessing the capabilities of the computer as a powerful research tool. The researcher in behavioral science must learn to use this tool or risk being left behind as his discipline advances [3, p. 4].

THE COMPUTER AND ITS FUNCTIONS

At the outset, we should like to make quite clear that we are not suggesting, nor would any computer scientist, that there is anything magical about the computer or that it is a panacea for all research problems. Given a desk calculator and a very large supply of pencils and paper, the individual researcher, working alone, could quite probably accomplish any single task that a computer could. But a computer can accomplish in sixty seconds what might take an individual several days to do; and in fifteen minutes, the computer can organize data and solve intricate mathematical problems that might take an individual, working full time, several weeks or even months to complete.

The computer can be described as "a high-speed clerk," performing various mathematical functions in time units measured in the millionths and even billionths of one second. The computer has the advantage of being able to handle great quantities of data, analyzing the material systematically (without error), and at the same time seek out patterns, relationships, and various combinations that might elude the individual researcher. (This means that the computer should be of especial interest to the content analyst. Certain aspects of content analysis can become quite tedious.)

What exactly is a computer? A computer is a high-speed calculating machine that performs arithmetic and logical operations on any given set of data in accordance with a specific set of instructions (a program) provided by the researcher. With proper programing, the computer can reduce raw data to sets of meaningful numbers through statistical analyses, and display these data in tables, columns, rows, or whatever format seems most useful.

For the content analyst, or for any behavioral researcher, Borko notes that the computer can contribute to any of the following three general functions:

a/ Organization and reduction of statistical data.
b/ Hypothesis seeking, by finding relationships.
c/ Hypothesis testing, through modeling and simulation [3, p. 5].

More specifically, the computer's basic operations are that (1) it can move numbers from one location to another inside the computer; (2) it can perform arithmetic operations – addition, subtraction, multiplication, division, and variations; (3) it can compare one quantity with another; and (4) it can control its own operation (limited of course to the programs, fixed and otherwise, for its operation). Figure 7 is a simple schematic diagram of a computer, drawn in terms of the operations just described.

Computer input consists of two basic elements – the program and the data to be processed in accordance with the program. The program is merely a specific list of instructions, written in one of several languages that can be processed by the computer (e.g., FORTRAN, ALGOL, and COMIT). The program governs the operations to be performed on the data – for example, computing mean scores, developing percentages, rank ordering data, executing tests of correlation, performing factor analyses, arranging the data for printing in a columnar table format. The data, of course, consist of the information gathered by the researcher, e.g., column inches, items, attention scores (more likely the raw data that will allow the computer to compute attention scores), or theme counts.

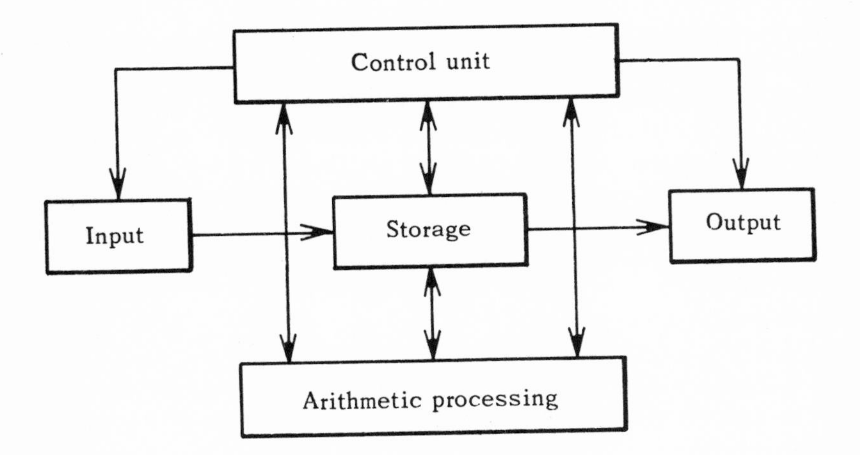

Figure 7/

The program and the data to be processed may be fed into the computer through one of several means. Most familiar to the student, probably, is the punched card. Information is transferred from coding sheets prepared by the analyst to data cards by a keypunch machine. The series of punches on a card are "read" by the computer as specific number or letter equivalents and are stored temporarily in the computer for processing. A variation of the punched card available to some computer systems is the mark-sensed card; data are entered on cards by marking the cards with a special pencil rather than by machine-punching holes into the cards. Either process is relatively simple to master, and if the equipment and materials are available, the analyst can carry out this phase of the work himself.

It is becoming more common and more convenient to feed data into the computer by magnetic tape. (Of course, the data must first be transferred to tape from cards or punched tape.) The plastic magnetic tape is much like that used in commercially sold tape recorders, except that it is somewhat larger and contains several channels for recording. Data are recorded on the tape in a series of electronic blips, which the computer translates in the same manner as it does the information contained on punched cards. Magnetic tape is increasing in popularity, because it makes possible higher input speed and large quantities of information can be stored on a single tape. Data contained on a tape can be easily updated, reusing the same portion of the tape. In most modern computer systems, tapes are used not only to input primary information into the computer, but also in tape banks to temporarily store certain data while the computer is solving problems.

Still another input device, which should be of particular interest to the content analyst, is punched paper tape – the same type of tape produced by a teletype for teletypesetting equipment. The paper tape is punched by regular typing; this means that the analyst has available not only the paper tape, but a typewritten copy of his input as well. If you are contemplating a content analysis of newspaper content, the standard teletype tape from the wire services can be adapted for direct computer input. If storage space were available, the entire content of a newspaper using TTS could be placed in computer storage for analysis.

In addition, most computer systems provide for direct input through a typewriter keyboard wired directly to the computer. However, this keyboard is not used extensively for input; it would take considerable time to enter a program and data for processing by this method. Normally, the keyboard provides computer operators a direct line of access in order to "talk" to (instruct) the computer while it is in operation.

At this point it is important to note that any of the input methods outlined can also receive output. For example, after the analyst's problem has been solved, he can if he desires, ask to have the results punched on cards or paper tape or stored on magnetic tape. In almost every case, once the computer has solved the computational problem, the results will be placed on magnetic tape, thus freeing the computer for other tasks. From there the data will be reproduced by a high-speed printer in a format that resembles typewriting.

Other means of loading information into a computer are being developed, but the most important one on the horizon for the content analyst is the optical scanner – a device that reads data into the computer directly from the printed page. While various models of optical scanners are in use for highly specialized and relatively simple material, a device that can read directly from a newspaper, book, or magazine has not yet been successfully developed for wide-scale use. When it is, the job of the content analyst will be greatly simplified.

APPLICATIONS IN CONTENT ANALYSIS

How you use the computer in content analysis studies, as in other forms of research, depends on the problem, the answers sought, and the general design of the study. After considering these factors, a general rationale for using computer analysis can be developed and some examples of how the computer was used in specific studies discussed.

One of the chief benefits of the computer, it seems to us, is that it can free the analyst from carrying out the tedious counting, sorting, identification, and analysis tasks inherent in most content studies, thus allowing him greater time for the further development of this research method. Where a researcher might previously have shied away from a more complex and perhaps more fruitful research design because of the sheer weight of the work involved, the computer provides the means of combating the tendency toward oversimplification. In the same vein, content analysts have in the past limited themselves to relatively small samples, again because of the great amount of work involved in analyzing large quantities of material. The computer provides the opportunity to use much larger samples of content, and perhaps increase the reliability of the results.

For the beginning researcher, two attributes of the computer should be particularly inviting: (1) the thoroughness with which the computer can read the material selected for analysis, thus eliminating the possibility of missing certain key symbols and (2) the accuracy with which the computer can do the necessary computational work – including sorting and categorizing, as well as arithmetic. If properly programed, then the computer can ensure a high degree of accuracy in your work.

From the standpoint of the content analyst, the computer can be used in two different ways. It can be used only for mathematic computations and ordering of data collected first by the researcher; or it can be used to actually analyze the content under study and at the same time perform related mathematic functions.

An example of the first instance can be provided by a study of Budd's [63], in which he analyzed the content of Australian and New Zealand daily newspapers from several different aspects. All the data abstracted from the sample of newspapers could have been recorded on data cards – e.g., category numbers (1 through 16), classification (favorable, neutral, unfavorable), length of the article, number of columns occupied by the headline, size of the accompanying picture, type of item (article, editorial, column, cartoon), placement on page. Employing a relatively simple program, Budd could have obtained the data used in his findings quite easily. The computer could have calculated total column inches in each category and the per cent of the total of all column inches that each category accounted for; rank order of categories for each newspaper, with accompanying correlation coefficients and significance levels; number of items in each category; etc. The attention score developed by Budd [62] as a measure of news prominence also could have been computed for each category and each newspaper using the relevant data on the cards. In addition, the computer could have been programed to output the findings in tabular form, thus solving the problem of organizing the data in tables. Of even greater importance to the beginning researcher, however, is the fact that the computer could have completed these tasks in approximately ten minutes, instead of the two months Budd, using a hand calculator and individual tabulation cards for every item, required.

The ability of the computer is not limited to figuring simple addition and determining percentages. The computer can just as easily (perhaps in a slightly longer time) conduct multiple linear-regression analysis, analysis of variance, factor analysis (orthogonal and oblique), and so on. With an adept programer, almost any statistical tool from the simple mean to the most complex factor analytic scheme can be adapted for computer usage.

We also stated that the computer can be used for actual analysis of content or written material. Normally, you might think the computer is able to work only numeric problems; in a sense, this is true. However, by converting letters to numbers, the computer can absorb and store words, sentences, paragraphs, etc. There are computer languages available to analyze material entered into the computer in such a manner. One such language, COMIT, has been developed by the Massachusetts Institute of Technology [19]. COMIT can be programed, for example, to check and correct spelling, word order, and punctuation; to insert or delete words; to seek out certain specified symbols and keep a count of their frequency of occurrence. There are many other computer languages available for processing language problems, some of them developed for use in only highly specialized problems. For example, many daily newspapers are using computers to set and justify type and to make certain corrections in incoming newspaper copy.

What kinds of research problems can be tackled with language-processing programs? Much depends on the computer facility available and the skill of the programer. Adams [259], at the University of North Carolina, developed a study comparing foreign and domestic news in a sample of American newspapers. The study was undertaken to examine four basic questions.

1/ Is foreign news more preoccupied with "soft" news than is domestic news?
2/ If foreign news treated as feature material more extensively than is domestic news?
3/ Is foreign news more sensational than domestic news?
4/ Is foreign news less detailed than domestic news?

Employing the Associated Press TA wire for the afternoon cycle as punched tape, Adams selected twenty days in a constructed month of weekdays (see Chapter 4). The twenty days amounted to eighty reels of punched tape. All eighty reels were fed into the computer, although it had been decided to analyze only the lead paragraphs and have them printed out for analysis. Using a content-scanning program developed by Danielson and Jackson [262], Adams ordered the computer to search for the symbols that appear in every Associated Press story, i.e., the (AP) logotype or the word "Associated." Upon encountering either of these two symbols, the computer backed up sixty characters and then transferred to magnetic tape the next 300 characters. In this manner, Adams isolated the datelines and the leads of every wire story. At the end of the computer run, all the leads were printed out in standard format.

Each of the leads was then analyzed by hand, employing a category system to provide the answers to the questions above. These data were recorded on coding sheets, punched on data cards, and run through the computer with a program that provided, in tables, whole numbers and percentages for each category, with a chi-square analysis and the attendant significance level.

Adams' study was not a complex one, yet the use of the computer at strategic points in the analysis saved considerable amounts of time and frustration—and perhaps contributed to the accuracy of the findings.

In Chapter 4 we discussed a unit for sampling content called the basic space unit (BSU) developed by Danielson and Mullen [83]. The two researchers developed a computer program for drawing BSU samples where the input consists of the name of the paper, number of issues, number of pages in each issue, and size of the sample of BSUs desired. The computer output from this program is a randomly generated list telling the researcher exactly what issue, what page, and where on the page the sample BSUs are located, thus saving considerable time in locating sample units. Such a program will reach full fruition when the contents of the newspapers can first be entered into the computer and the sample basic space units selected and printed out for analysis, similar to the manner in which Adams got his printout of newspaper-article leads. At this writing, a solution to this step is still being sought.

Tannenbaum and Brewer [236] of the University of Wisconsin's Mass Communications Research Center adapted a computer program to a study of the consistency of syntactic structure as a factor in journalistic style. The program they employed searches content and places each word in a designated passage into its proper grammatic category. The program accomplishes this in three ways: first, by checking the word against a dictionary list stored in the computer's memory; second, by categorizing the remaining words on the basis of affixes that are listed in dictionary fashion in the computer; and third, by assigning all remaining unidentified words through a probability scheme on the basis of the grammatic environment. Such programing techniques show great promise for the eventual execution of content analyses almost completely through the use of the computer.

Budd and Trayes of the University of Iowa's Mass Communication Research Bureau applied factor analysis and Q analysis (see Chapter 9) to learn more about news mix proportions of various categories of news and cyclic trends. Data for the analysis were collected by standard methods, assigning column inches to twenty-two news categories over a thirty-one-day period. After keypunching the data, the first phase of the operation was completed with two separate computer runs: the intercorrelation of news items and the intercorrelation of days by news items. The intercorrelation of items produced several clusters which were subsequently linked with the number of pages per issue, among other possibilities, indicating that certain categories vary with the space available while others do not. The intercorrelation of news mix and days indicated that Q factor analysis – designating the various issues of the newspaper as treatments and the news categories as items – would be fruitful. The resultant analysis produced a three-factor solution, indicating that similar patterns of news presentation existed on certain days: factor I, on Sundays and Mondays; factor II, on Tuesdays, Fridays and Saturdays; factor III, on Thursdays. Employing a procedure called *weighted rotational analysis procedure* (WRAP), which produces a listing of news categories ordered in descending array according to Z-score weights for each of the factors, the answer was found to the question: Why are the days listed within factors similar in pattern, and what makes the factors unlike each other?

Additional possibilities for this type of study are to analyze such categories in terms of attention scores, to compare several papers from several countries, or to compare wire service output with actual usage. This kind of experimentation has only begun, and will be limited only by the imagination of those seeking new and significant ways of using the computer in content analysis.

THE COMPUTER AND YOUR STUDY

If you have not yet been exposed to computers, their use and physical appearance, pay a visit to your university computer center or the computer installation through which you might work. If you are contemplating using a computer in your content study, seek out a professional programer at your computer facility and discuss your research design with him. He will be able to show you methods of organization that will make electronic processing of your data more efficient. Because of the different research designs with which he has worked, he may even be able to show you how you can strengthen your study as a whole.

The most important phase of the computer operation as far as you are concerned will be the organization and coding of your data so that it can be efficiently transferred to punch cards. Most computer centers will provide, either free or at a nominal cost, coding sheets numbered in the same manner as the data cards used in that center. Each blank on the sheet will be filled with an entry for each column on the data card. The researcher merely enters the appropriate number in each blank, and the cards are easily punched directly from the coding sheets.

Before you begin your coding, however, you should make up a set of coding instructions that tell you what variable you have placed in which column and that provide a clear identification of the coding system used (what does each number mean?). In your coding instructions, include any other notes to yourself that seem important. There is nothing quite so useless as a deck of punched data cards without some knowledge of what the punches represent. The few minutes required to make up a set of coding instructions will save headaches later on.

Do you think the computer too complex or too sophisticated for your level at this point? Because the use of the computer in the behavioral sciences is relatively new, even experienced communication researchers have to face this situation. John B. Adams, whose study we cited earlier, shares his experience about his first use of the computer.

> There is an aura about computers that tends to make us shy away from them — all except some of the daring pioneers. I had been aware of their utility in a lot of fields, but this study is the first in which I felt the urge to try it myself.
>
> I know nothing about computer programming — I stand in awe as the 1105A hums away. But it is true on our campus — and I am sure on most of yours, too — that there are many persons working on the computers who not only know what the machines are all about, but who are more than willing to take the time to explain to novices and to help them take advantage of the machine's ability to do things quickly and accurately. Take it from a novice who found out — it IS worth looking into [258, p. 8].

If your study looks as though it might be made easier if you have the computations and analysis done while you wait, by all means let the computer do it.

In addition to the literature cited earlier in this chapter, a book by Stone and his associates* offers an important approach to computer content analysis. Their computer program provides procedures through which recurrent patterns of communication (oral or written) can be identified. The program accepts test material, has a dictionary system for ease in locating data, counts occurrences, and retrieves specified content.

*Phillip J. Stone et al., *The General Inquirer: A Computer Approach to Content Analysis* (Cambridge, Mass.: The Massachusetts Institute of Technology Press), 1966.

bibliography

Bibliography items are listed under four main headings: books, articles, papers and monographs, theses and dissertations. Items are listed alphabetically by author under each heading. However, the numbering of items is consecutive throughout the entire Bibliography.

BOOKS

1/ Ackoff, Russell L.: *The Design of Social Research* (Chicago: The University of Chicago Press), 1953. While this book is not directed at content analysis research, the procedures discussed are generally applicable to quantitative research designs.

2/ Berelson, Bernard: *Content Analysis in Communication Research* (New York: The Free Press of Glencoe), 1952. The first, and in many respects the most complete, treatment available on techniques, rationale, and uses of content analysis as a research tool; but it does not emphasize the emerging view of content analysis as a tool for observing behavior.

3/ Borko, Harold: *Computer Applications in the Behavioral Sciences* (Englewood Cliffs, N.J.: Prentice-Hall, Inc.), 1962. Like the Cooley and Lohnes book listed below, it discusses use of computers in statistical analysis. History, basic introductory material, illustrated.

4/ Brooks, Maxwell R.: *The Negro Press Re-Examined: Political Content of Leading Negro Newspapers* (Boston: Christopher Publishing House), 1959. This is the application of content analysis to the study of political material in United Stages Negro newspapers. A stabilized list of symbols is used. This study suggests that content analysis might be used to study other sections of the Negro press. The study should be updated because 1948 issues are used and there has been much change since in areas of significance to the Negro.

5/ Bross, Irwin D. J.: "Models," in James H. Campbell and Hal W. Hepler (eds.), *Dimensions in Communication* (Belmont, California: Wadsworth), 1965. Provides a model for looking at and conceptualizing the use of models.

6/ Campbell, James H., and Hal W. Hepler (eds.): *Dimensions in Communication* (Belmont, California: Wadsworth), 1965. The underlying thesis of this collection of writings is that persuasion exists in all communication. The collection is organized in four general sections: conceptual frames, persuasion, language, writing.

7/ Cartwright, Dorwin P.: "Analysis of Qualitative Material," in Leon Festinger and Daniel Katz (eds.), *Research Methods in the Behavioral Sciences* (New York: Holt, Rinehart and Winston, Inc.), 1953. It provides illustrations for types of content analyses described by Berelson. It raises the question of the significance of analyses and offers an outline for doing analysis.

8/ Cooley, William W., and Paul R. Lohnes: *Multivariate Procedures for the Behavioral Sciences* (New York: John Wiley & Sons, Inc.), 1962. Procedures are described in terms of their use with computer programs, which are also included.

9/ Danielson, Wayne: "Content Analysis in Communication Research," in Ralph O. Nafziger and David Manning White (eds.), *Introduction to Mass Communications Research* (Baton Rouge, La.: Louisiana State University Press), 1963. Some of the current uses of content analysis are discussed. It is an excellent capsule summary of the method.

10/ Deutschmann, Paul J.: "Measurement in Communication Research," in Ralph O. Nafziger and David Manning White (eds.) *Introduction to Mass Communications Research* (Baton Rouge, La.: Louisiana State University Press), 1963. Stresses measurement of variables contributing to change as a requisite for significant research. Explains unidimensional and multidimensional measurement, problems of reliability and validity, and use of Guttman scale and semantic differential.

11/ Deutschmann, Paul J.: *News-Page Content of Twelve Metropolitan Dailies* (Cincinnati: Scripps-Howard Research), 1959. Studies every other weekday issue for four weeks of seven New York, three Cleveland and two Cincinnati dailies. Tests usefulness of news categories developed by Freyschlag. Applies linkage analysis to news categories to determine emphasis clusters.

12/ Dovring, Karin: "Land Reform as a Propaganda Theme, a Study in Quantitative Semantics," in Folke Dovring (ed.), *Land and Labor in Europe in the Twentieth Century* (The Hague, Netherlands: Martinus Nijhoff), 1965. See also Appendix 7.

13/ Edwards, Allen L.: *Statistical Methods for the Behavioral Sciences* (New York: Holt, Rinehart and Winston, Inc.), 1954. A broad text covering basic mathematical functions, statistical concepts, and both parametric and nonparametric techniques.

14/ Festinger, Leon, and Daniel Katz (eds.): *Research Methods in the Behavioral Sciences* (New York: The Dryden Press, Inc.), 1953. A good general reference for the student of behavioral science.

15/ George, Alexander L.: *Propaganda Analysis* (Evanston, Ill.: Row, Peterson & Company), 1959. Examines predictions and inferences made from Nazi mass communication material by Allied analysts, particularly American. Contrasts direct and indirect inference and frequency and nonfrequency analysis.

16/ Goode, William J., and Paul K. Hatt: *Methods in Social Research* (New York: McGraw-Hill Book Company), 1952. A standard text with sections bearing directly on content analysis as well as discussions of methods adaptable to content analysis.

17/ Guttman, Louis: "A New Approach to Factor Analysis: The Radex," in Paul F. Lazarsfeld (ed.), *Mathematical Thinking in the Social Sciences* (New York: The Free Press of Glencoe), 1954. An approach, opening the way to prediction, involving the simplex and the circumplex. Implications for content analysis and trends in content.

18/ Handel, Leo A.: *Hollywood Looks at Its Audience* (Urbana, Ill.: The University of Illinois Press), 1950. Contains a chapter which summarizes and defines previous work in the content analysis of motion pictures.

19/ *An Introduction to COMIT programming* (Cambridge: The Massachusetts Institute of Technology Press), 1963. Comprehensive instructions in the use of the COMIT language. Also available from the same source is the *COMIT Programmer's Reference Manual.*

20/ Jonassen, Christen T.: *The Measurement of Community Dimensions and Elements* (Columbus, Ohio: Ohio State University Press), 1959. Using counties as his communal units, Jonassen developed measures and ranked each of Ohio's eighty-eight counties on each of eighty-three dimensions of community lite from data available in the United States Census and other reports.

21/ Kerlinger, Fred N.: *Foundations of Behavioral Research* (New York: Holt, Rinehart and Winston, Inc.), 1964. Discusses content analysis as a means for observing behavior. Includes descriptions of techniques and procedures which may be used in content studies involving other variables.

22/ Kish, Leslie: "Selection of the Sample," in Leon Festinger and Daniel Katz (eds.), *Research Methods in the Behavioral Sciences* (New York: The Dryden Press, Inc.), 1953. Introductory explanation of simple random stratification and cluster sampling theory, techniques, and problems.

23/ Lasswell, Harold D., Nathan Leites, and Associates (eds.): *Language of Politics* (South Norwalk, Conn.: George W. Stewart, Publisher, Inc.), 1949. This collection of essays by leading content analysts covers many phases of research.

24/ Lasswell, Harold D., Daniel Lerner, and Ithiel deSola Pool: *The Comparative Study of Symbols* (Stanford, Calif.: Stanford University Press), 1952. A summary of content analysis theory as it relates to political symbols and symbolic analysis in general. The book summarizes methods of research to data with emphasis on verbal symbols.

25/ Lazarsfeld, Paul F.: "Interpretation of Statistical Relations as a Research Operation," in Paul F. Lazarsfeld and Morris Rosenberg (eds.), *The Language of Social Research* (New York: The Free Press of Glencoe), 1955. A technical explanation of a formula for testing for a causal or spurious relationship between two variables by introducing a third. The approach can be extended to *n* variables.

26/ Lazarsfeld, Paul F., Bernard Berelson, and Hazel Gaudet: *The People's Choice: How the Voter Makes Up His Mind in a Presidential Campaign* (New York: Columbia University Press), 1944. Chapter 13 contains specific information on the classification of direction (direction within direction).

27/ MacLean, Malcolm S., Jr.: "Research Planning," in Ralph O. Nafziger and David Manning White (eds.), *Introduction to Mass Communications Research* (Baton Rouge, La.: Louisiana State University Press), 1963. Levels and planning of research projects in clear and direct language. An excellent starting place for the beginning researcher.

28/ MacLean, Malcolm S., Jr.: "Systems of News Communication," in Lee Thayer (ed.), *Communication: Theory and Practice* (Springfield, Ill.: Charles C. Thomas, Publisher), 1966. Suggestions for the application of general systems theory and *Q* methodology in communication research.

29/ North, Robert C., Ole Holsti, M. George Zaninovich, and Dina A. Zinnes: *Content Analysis: A Handbook with Applications for the Study of International Crisis* (Evanston Ill.: Northwestern University Press), 1963. It includes an especially interesting chapter on computer use in content analysis. Special application for analysis of political documents.

30/ Osgood, Charles E., George J. Suci, and Percy H. Tannenbaum: *The Measurement of Meaning* (Urbana, Ill.: University of Illinois Press), 1957. This is the major work in which the authors cite factors involved in the measurement of meaning and the development of the semantic differential.

31/ Pool, Ithiel deSola: *Trends in Content Analysis* (Urbana, Ill.: The University of Illinois Press), 1959. Composed of comments by several authors who participated in a seminar on content analysis, this book is in effect a survey of several developments since the publication of Berelson's study.

32/ Schramm, Wilbur: "The Challenge to Communication Research," in Ralph O. Nafziger and David Manning White (eds.), *Introduction to Communication Research* (Baton Rouge, La.: Louisiana State University Press), 1963. Describes general areas of communication research.

33/ Schramm, Wilbur: "The Gatekeeper: A Memorandum," in Wilbur Schramm (ed.), *Mass Communications* (Urbana, Ill.: The University of Illinois Press), 1960. Discusses the gatekeeper role in the mass media.

34/ Siegal, Sidney: *Nonparametric Statistics for the Behavioral Sciences* (New York: McGraw-Hill Book Company), 1956. A useful aid for conducting nonparametric tests on data. Useful not only for its explanations of statistical tests but also for general statements about research methods and testing hypotheses. Good discussion of measurement.

35/ Smith, Alfred (ed.): *Culture and Communication* (New York: Holt, Rinehart and Winston, Inc.), 1966. Fifty-five current studies from several disciplines present a picture of the communication process from four general areas: theory, syntactics, semantics, and pragmatics.

36/ Smith, Bruce L., Harold D. Lasswell, and Ralph D. Casey: *Propaganda, Communication, and Public Opinion* (Princeton, N.J.: Princeton University Press), 1946. Includes Lasswell's essay "Describing the Contents of Communications," an introductory piece about manifest content description of all media.

37/ Stephenson, William: *The Study of Behavior* (Chicago: The University of Chicago Press), 1953. The basic source for the study of Stephenson's *Q* methodology, exposition, data collection by *Q* sort, analysis, and interpretation.

38/ Westley, Bruce H., and Malcolm S. MacLean, Jr., "A Conceptual Model for Communication Research," in Campbell and Hepler [6] and Smith [35]. Originally published in *Journalism Quarterly*, vol. 34, no. 1, pp. 31–38, 1957. Based on earlier work by Westley and MacLean in *Audio-Visual Communications Review*, vol. 3, no. 1, pp. 3–12, 1955, and "Research on 'Fortuitous' Communication: A Review," *Audio-Visual Communications Review*, vol. 3, no. 2, pp. 119–137, 1955. See also entry 250 in this bibliography.

39/ Wolenstein, Martha, and Nathan Leites: *Movies: A Psychological Study* (New York: The Free Press of Glencoe), 1950. A psychological examination of films from three cultures: English, French, and American.

ARTICLES

40/ Abu-Lughod, Ibrahim: "International News in the Arabic Press: A Comparative Content Analysis," *Public Opinion Quarterly*, vol. 26, no. 4, pp. 600–612, 1962. The press in seven Arab states is discussed in terms of foreign news content. Weighted attitude scales reveal ambivalence and diversity in the treatment of world powers.

41/ Adams, John B.: "What the Foreign Correspondent Does for a Newspaper's Readers," *Journalism Quarterly*, vol. 43, no. 4, pp. 300–304, 1966. The content of newspapers with foreign correspondents as compared to those without correspondents is treated quantitatively and qualitatively.

42/ Albrecht, Milton C.: "Does Literature Reflect Common Values?" *American Sociological Review*, vol. 21, no. 6, pp. 722–729, 1956. Excellent example of sociological analysis of mass media content. Purposive sampling of magazines to analyze fiction.

43/ Alisky, Marvin: "The Peruvian Press and the Nixon Incident," *Journalism Quarterly*, vol. 35, no. 4, pp. 411–419, 1958. Nonquantitative analysis of daily newspapers in regard to a specific issue.

44/ Auster, Donald: "Content Analysis in AV Communication Research," *Audio Visual Communication Review,* vol. 4, no. 2, pp. 102–108, 1956. Applications of techniques to the virtually neglected field of instructional materials. Selected bibliography of content analysis of various media.

45/ Backer, Jack E.: "The 'Prestige Press' and News Management in the Cuban Crisis," *Journalism Quarterly,* vol. 41, no. 2, pp. 264–265, 1964. News management items analyzed as favorable or unfavorable and intensity of direction determined in this study of the editorial pages of thirteen leading United States newspapers. The time period is the five days in 1962 following the news conference of President Kennedy in which he admitted that some news had been managed.

46/ Backman, Carl W.: "Sampling Mass Media Content: The Use of the Cluster Design," *American Sociological Review,* vol. 21, no. 6, pp. 729–733, 1956. Discusses cluster sampling in a study of mass media content; cites the advantages of reduced costs and time.

47/ Barcus, Francis E.: "Advertising in the Sunday Comics," *Journalism Quarterly,* vol. 39, no. 2, pp. 196–202, 1962. What is advertised, and by what methods, in the Sunday comics section. This study reports on the volume and content of such advertising in 1947 and 1955 (after the impact of television had been felt).

48/ Barcus, Francis E.: "A Content Analysis of Trends in Sunday Comics, 1900–1959," *Journalism Quarterly,* vol. 38, no. 2, pp. 171–180, 1961. This study classifies comic strips in several ways – by types, formulas, themes, and subjects.

49/ Barnes, Arthur M.: "Research in Radio and Television News," *Journalism Quarterly,* vol. 34, no. 3, pp. 323–332, 1957. A summary of studies of the content of broadcast news is given in a sub-section ("What is available to the audience?").

50/ Barnes, Arthur M., and Paul Lyness: "How the Wire Services Reported the Rutledge Murder Trial: A Study in Taste," *Journalism Quarterly,* vol. 28, no. 2, pp. 161–178, 1951. Combines content analysis and personal interviewing.

51/ Batlin, Robert: "San Francisco Newspapers' Campaign Coverage 1896, 1952," *Journalism Quarterly,* vol. 31, no. 3, pp. 297–302, 1954. Seeks to determine political bias using direction categories favorable, neutral, and unfavorable.

52/ Bend, Emil: "Marriage Offers in a Yiddish Newspaper – 1935 and 1950," *American Journal of Sociology,* vol. 58, no. 1, pp. 60–66, 1952. Tabulates data under thirteen personal characteristics divided into four sets of characteristics: female-own qualities, female-desired, male-own, and male-desired.

53/ Berkman, Dave: "Advertising in *Ebony* and *Life:* Negro Aspiration vs. Reality," *Journalism Quarterly,* vol. 40, no. 1, pp. 53–64, 1963. The advertising in nineteen categories is seen as quantitatively and qualitatively different in the two magazines. Differences in appeals are exemplified by different brands, model complexions, etc.

54/ Bogart, Leo: "Magazines Since the Rise of Television," *Journalism Quarterly,* vol. 33, no. 2, pp. 153–166, 1956. Classifies content in three main categories – High Brow, Middle Brow, and Below Middle – with a number of subcategories under each.

55/ Bonjean, Charles M., Richard J. Hill, and Dale S. McLemore: "Continuities in Measurement," *Social Forces,* vol. 43, no. 4, pp. 522–532, 1965. Content analysis on all issues of four leading sociological journals for a five-year period indicates a lack of agreement and research continuity with respect to the use of measurement procedures.

56/ Bostian, Lloyd R., and John E. Ross: "Functions and Meanings of Mass Media for Wisc. Farm Women," *Journalism Quarterly,* vol. 42, no. 1, pp. 69–76, 1965. Projective tests, direct questions, and inferred functions are applied as measures to analyze women's attitudes to media.

57/ Brandner, Lowell, and Joan Sistrunk: "The Newspaper; Molder or Mirror of Community Values?" *Journalism Quarterly,* vol. 43, no. 3, pp. 497–505, 1966. Analysis of the way education is reported in newspaper stories and the education levels in the corresponding counties.

58/ Breed, Warren: "Comparative Newspaper Handling of the Emmett Till Case," *Journalism Quarterly,* vol. 35, no. 3, pp. 291–298, 1958. Thematic analysis of eleven Negro and white newspapers from North and South. Themes used to uncover stereo types.

59/ Breed, Warren: "Mass Communication and Socio-Cultural Integration," *Social Forces,* vol. 37, no. 2, pp. 109–116, 1958. Reverse content analysis – data gathered from published reports of community research, reported examples of media suppression of news.

Omissions classified by "areas of protection" (including business elites, religion, and doctors).

60/ Broom, Leonard, and Shirley Reece: "Political and Racial Interest: A Study in Content Analysis," *Public Opinion Quarterly*, vol. 19, no. 1, pp. 5–19, 1955. Selects ten symbols for quantitative and qualitative analysis (e.g., Jim Crow, legal lynching, all-white jury, left wing, and Communist). Classifies data into three main themes – denial of civil rights, racial discrimination, and subversive contamination. Each theme is judged on basis of frequency of key symbols.

61/ Bryan, Carter R.: "Communist Advertising: Its Status and Function," *Journalism Quarterly*, vol. 39, no. 4, pp. 500-506, 1962. Trend analysis of advertising in the Soviet Union and other Communist countries.

62/ Budd, Richard W.: "Attention Score: A Device for Measuring News 'Play'," *Journalism Quarterly*, vol. 41, no. 2, pp. 259–262, 1964. An attention score is developed and used for analysis of United States news in eight Australian and New Zealand dailies.

63/ Budd, Richard W.: "U.S. News in the Press Down Under," *Public Opinion Quarterly*, vol. 28, no. 1, pp. 39–56, 1964. An analysis of Australian and New Zealand newspapers undertaken to find out what was being said about the United States and how it was being said. This quantitative analysis of eight publications measures space in terms of column inches, counts items, and uses the attention score.

64/ Bunn, Ronald F.: The Spiegel Affair and the West German Press: The Initial Phase," *Public Opinion Quarterly*, vol. 30, no. 1, pp. 33–54, 1966. Content analysis to study West German press reaction to the arrest by West German authorities of the editors of the magazine *Der Spiegel* for allegedly traitorously revealing state secrets.

65/ Bush, Chilton R.: "The Analysis of Political Campaign News," *Journalism Quarterly*, vol. 28, no. 2, pp. 250–252, 1951. Content analysis based on themes and measurement of column inches. Includes specific definitions of how direction – favorable, unfavorable, and neutral – is to be determined.

66/ Bush, Chilton R.: "A System of Categories for General News Content," *Journalism Quarterly*, vol. 37, no. 2, pp. 206–210, 1960. A listing of fifty subject categories, including definitions, for the classification of newspaper content. These categories lend themselves to expansion or condensation.

67/ Carter, Roy E.: "Segregation and the News: A Regional Content Study," *Journalism Quarterly,* vol. 34, no. 1, pp. 3-18, 1957. This analysis of the content of selected newspapers tends to support charges that the southern press is inattentive to desegregation. The study employs broad subject categories and direction classifications.

68/ Casey, Ralph D., and Thomas D. Copland: "Use of Foreign News in 19 Minnesota Dailies," *Journalism Quarterly,* vol. 35, no. 1, pp. 87-89, 1958. An approach to the study of foreign news content.

69/ Cattell, Raymond B.: "The Three Basic Factor-Analytic Research Designs – Their Interrelations and Derivatives," *Psychological Bulletin,* vol. 49, no. 5, pp. 499–520, 1952. Defines the six primary factor-analytic experimental designs and reduces these to three independent common-matrix pairs, showing their separate and interrelated uses.

70/ Christenson, Reo M.: "Report on the Reader's Digest," *Columbia Journalism Review,* vol. 3, no. 4, pp. 30–36, 1965. Public affairs articles in the *Digest* for the last twenty years are analyzed by a man who is a political scientist and former newspaperman. His analysis is that the articles reflect "avowedly conservative" philosopy – pro-Republican, anti-Federal government. He continues his judgment by claiming that articles include repeated distortion and misinformation. It would be most interesting to have someone else do a content analysis of the same *Digest* articles and to compare results.

71/ Clarke, Peter, and Virginia Esposito: "A Study of Occupational Advice for Women in Magazines," *Journalism Quarterly,* vol. 43, no. 3, pp. 477–485, 1966. Content analysis combined with other research techniques. Content categories derived mostly from motivation theory are applied to women's magazines' articles about occupations for women. Also, a sample of college women *Q*-sorted magazine statements into the content categories. Study shows a wide gulf between editors' "perspectives on work and the values shared by many of their readers."

72/ Colby, R. N., George A. Collier, and Susan K. Postal: "Comparison of Themes in Folktales by the General Inquirer System," *Journal of American Folklore,* vol. 76, no. 302, pp. 318–323, 1963. Uses an IBM 2090 for counting words constituting the various themes to be analyzed. Clusters of themes are considered insights into cultures. The study lists 180 computer themes and sample entries.

73/ Conrad, Richard: "Social Images in East and West Germany: A

Comparative Study of Matched Newspapers in Two Social Systems,'' *Social Forces,* vol. 33, no. 3, pp. 281–285, 1955. The general method of study is comparative content analysis of representative and available daily and weekly newspapers published in East and West Berlin. Uses paired samples.

74/ Cony, Edward R.: ''Conflict-Cooperation Content of Five American Dailies,'' *Journalism Quarterly,* vol. 30, no. 1, pp. 15–22, 1953. Categories designed to cover all news content that could be considered relational. Subjective judgments had to be made frequently in classifying news content.

75/ Cooper, Eunice, and Helen Dinerman: ''Analysis of the Film 'Don't be a Sucker','' *Public Opinion Quarterly,* vol. 15, no. 2, pp. 243–265, 1951. Valuable for method approach. Authors divide research into two phases: (1) qualitative judgments of results from the film based upon interviews and questionnaires and (2) quantitative phases in which the magnitude of these results are measured.

76/ Cornwell, Elmer E.: ''Presidential News: The Expanding Public Image,'' *Journalism Quarterly,* vol. 36, no. 3, pp. 275-283, 1959. An analysis of front-page news over seventy years, indicating increase in presidential news. Example of single-subject content analysis.

77/ Cornwell, Elmer E.: ''The Press Conferences of Woodrow Wilson,'' *Journalism Quarterly,* vol. 39, no. 3, pp. 292-300, 1962. The author examines President Wilson's relations with the press by analyzing fifty-seven transcripts of Wilson's news conferences.

78/ Crane, Edgar, and Malcolm S. MacLean, Jr.: ''Five Dimensions of Style in Educational TV Programs,'' *Audio Visual Communication Review,* vol. 10, no. 3, pp. 158–168, 1962. Kinescopes of twenty educational TV programs are studied for personalization, verbal difficulty, verbosity, visual and auditory materials and methods. A study of audiences included.

79/ Cutlip, Scott M.: ''Content and Flow of AP News – from Trunk to TTS to Reader,'' *Journalism Quarterly,* vol. 31, no. 4, pp. 434–446, 1954. Detailed categorization of news content from American wire services.

80/ Danielson, Wayne, and John B. Adams: ''Completeness of Press Coverage of the 1960 Campaign,'' *Journalism Quarterly,* vol. 38, no. 4, pp. 441–452, 1961. Using a sample of ninety dailies with reference to twenty-three campaign events, the completeness of coverage of these events is studied.

81/ Danielson, Wayne, and Sam Dunn Bryan, "Computer Automation of Two Readability Formulas," *Journalism Quarterly,* vol. 40, no. 2, pp. 201–205, 1963. Describes difficulties in adapting Flesch readability formula for use by computers.

82/ Danielson, Wayne, and Sam Dunn Bryan, "Readability of Wire Stories in Eight News Categories," *Journalism Quarterly,* vol. 41, no. 1, pp. 105–106, 1964. Uses computer readability formulas to check readability of different news categories.

83/ Danielson, Wayne, and James J. Mullen, "A Basic Space Unit for Newspaper Content Analysis," *Journalism Quarterly,* vol. 42, no. 1, pp. 108–110, 1965. More complete studies of larger samples of newspaper content over a longer period of time is given as the basic advantage of the basic space unit (BSU). Its development and use is explained in this report, which also lists a number of disadvantages of the BSU.

84/ Dasbach, Anita Mallinckrodt: "U.S.-Soviet Magazine Propaganda: *America Illustrated* and *USSR,*" *Journalism Quarterly,* vol. 43, no. 1, pp. 73–84, 1966. The nature and effectiveness of United States-Soviet propaganda is studied within the context of changing East-West relations. Contents of 1960 and 1963 issues of the two propaganda magazines are analyzed.

85/ Davis, E. James: "Crime News in Colorado Newspapers," *American Journal of Sociology,* vol. 57, no. 4, pp. 325–330, 1952. Davis samples issues of four newspapers, drawing every sixth day. He experiments with different sampling procedures, using each paper, and finds no significant difference between means of final method and census of two months of papers. He combines the results of content analysis with the results of public opinion poll.

86/ Davis, E. James, and Lester W. Turner: "Sample Efficiency in Quantitative Newspaper Content Analysis," *Public Opinion Quarterly,* vol. 15, no. 4, pp. 762–763, 1952. The authors use every sixth day to create a sample for a study of crime news in Colorado daily newspapers. They use the same days for each month after applying the sixth day procedure in January, using January 1 as the first day for the procedure.

87/ Davis, Hal, and Galen Rarick: "Functions of Editorials and Letters to the Editor," *Journalism Quarterly,* vol. 41, no. 1, pp. 108–109, 1964. An analysis of editorials and reader comment in twenty-one Oregon dailies on the issue of whether a known Communist should be allowed to speak at state-supported colleges and universities.

88/ Davis, John A.: "Superimposition of Supplemental Information on an Instructional Film," *Audio Visual Communication Review,* vol. 13, no. 3, pp. 275–288, 1965. Analysis of scene content and length in order to hold each constant for a study of two different films.

89/ DeFleur, Melvin L.: "Occupational Roles as Portrayed on Television," *Public Opinion Quarterly,* vol. 28, no. 1, pp. 57–74, 1964. The televised portrayals of occupations are studied with special procedures to examine the occupational roles presented, the settings in which they are shown, and the characteristics of workers as portrayed in the roles.

90/ Dollard, John, and O. H. Mowrer: "A Method of Measuring Tension in Written Documents," *Journal of Abnormal Psychology,* vol. 42, no. 4, pp. 3–32, 1947. Recommends use of discomfort-relief quotient as a means of structuring content for analysis.

91/ Donohew, Lewis: "Decoder Behavior on Incongruent Political Material: A Pilot Study," *Journal of Communication,* vol. 16, no. 2, pp. 133–142, 1966. The author uses cloze procedure to study comprehension by politically active and politically inactive readers of good news and bad news about a candidate.

92/ Donohew, Lewis: "Newspaper Gatekeepers and Forces in the News Channel," *Public Opinion Quarterly,* vol. 31, no. 1, 1967. Combines content analysis, attitude measurement, and demographic data to determine the relationship of newspaper coverage of an issue to publisher attitude, perceived community opinion, and community conditions that might be related to the issue.

93/ Dovring, Karin: "Propaganda for America: The Rockefeller Panel Reports," *American Behavioral Scientist,* vol. 4, no. 9, pp. 31–37, 1961. Analyzes the six Rockefeller panel reports for three kinds of symbols – those presenting values accepted by the American community and identified with, those expressing problems that menace continued existence of the community, and those referring to demands that might solve these problems.

94/ Dunning, John L.: "The Kennedy Assassination As Viewed by Communist Media," *Journalism Quarterly,* vol. 41, no. 2, pp. 163–169, 1964. An account of Communist-media coverage of President Kennedy's assassination gathered from monitoring reports on Soviet Russia, East European, and other Communist broadcasts and publications.

95/ Edelstein, Alex A., and Alan Ping-lin Liu: "Anti-Americanism in Red China's *People's Daily:* A Functional Analysis," *Jour-*

nalism Quarterly, vol. 40, no. 2, pp. 187–195, 1963. An analysis of the image of the United States presented in a Red Chinese daily during 1959. The analysis is a clarification of methods and themes of the propaganda efforts of the Red Chinese.

96/ Edelstein, Alex A., and J. Blaine Schulz: "The Weekly Newspaper's Leadership Role as Seen by Community Leaders," *Journalism Quarterly,* vol. 40, no. 4, pp. 565–574, 1963. See also the study by Alex A. Edelstein and Joseph Contris, "The Public View of the Weekly Newspaper's Leadership Role," *Journalism Quarterly,* vol. 43, no. 1, pp. 17–24, 1966.

97/ Ellison, Jerome, and Franklin T. Gosser: "Non-Fiction Magazine Articles: A Content Analysis Study," *Journalism Quarterly,* vol. 36, no. 1, pp. 27–34, 1959. Traces changes in subject matter, writing style, and article length for individual magazines and compiles data for entire sample, 1947–1959.

98/ Evans, James F.: Agricultural News in Illinois Daily Newspapers," *Journalism Quarterly,* vol. 43, no. 1, pp. 124–129, 1966. Personal interviews and year-long content analysis regarding the use of agricultural news during a period of time in which the Illinois farm population comprised only 6 per cent of the total population of the state.

99/ Exline, Ralph V., and Barbara H. Long: "An Application of Psychological Scaling Methods to Content Analysis: The Use of Empirically Derived Criterion Weights to Improve Intercoder Reliability," *Journal of Applied Psychology,* vol. 49, no. 22, pp. 142–149, 1965. The title is self-explanatory.

100/ Fosdick, James A., and Percy H. Tannenbaum: "The Encoder's Intent and Use of Stylistic Elements in Photographs," *Journalism Quarterly,* vol. 41, no. 2, pp. 175–182, 1964. An experimental study of photographs with the intent of the encoder as the independent variable. Discussion of process and stylistic variables in photographs.

101/ Foster, Schuler: "How America Became Belligerent: A Quantitative Study of War News, 1914–1917," *American Journal of Sociology,* vol. 40, no. 4, pp. 464–476, 1935. Uses *The New York Times* to show "that the crisis that led immediately to our entry into the war was the final one in a series of crises of ever-increasing intensity."

102/ Gardner, Leroy W.: "A Content Analysis of Japanese and American Television," *Journal of Broadcasting,* vol. 6, no. 1, pp. 45–52, 1962. Compares television logs for a ninety-day period, separating programs into five-minute units. Includes categories for television programs.

103/ Garver, Richard A.: "Content of Korean Language Daily Newspapers," *Gazette,* vol. 8, no. 4, pp. 302–316, 1962. A detailed study of the content of Korean newspapers including form, style, origin, and subject of items.

104/ Garver, Richard A.: "The Labor Press as a Leadership Tool," *Journalism Quarterly,* vol. 35, no. 3, pp. 324–332, 1958. This content analysis indicates that the labor publications sampled had the primary mission of selling the organization and its leaders to the workers. Details of coding-reliability check.

105/ Garver, Richard A.: "Polite Propaganda: *USSR* and *America Illustrated,*" *Journalism Quarterly,* vol. 38, no. 4, pp. 480–484, 1961. A considerable difference in emphasis is indicated by this content analysis of the first-year issues of the two propaganda magazines.

106/ Geller, A., D. Kaplan, and Harold Lasswell: "An Experimental Comparison of Four Ways of Coding Editorial Content,"*Journalism Quarterly,* vol. 19, no. 4, pp. 362–370, 1942. Basic methods and considerations in content analysis of newspapers. Deals primarily with methods of coding editorial content.

107/ Gerbner, George: "Ideological Perspectives and Political Tendencies in News Reporting," *Journalism Quarterly,* vol. 41, no. 4, pp. 494–508, 1964. A proposition analysis is developed and employed to measure differences in content of a criminal case in the French press by different sources.

108/ Gerbner, George: "Press Perspectives in World Communication: A Pilot Study," *Journalism Quarterly,* vol. 38, no. 3, pp. 313–322, 1961. Content analysis of headlines to determine the differences between conflict-oriented and substantive-oriented papers.

109/ Gieber, Walter: "Across the Desk: A Study of 16 Telegraph Editors," *Journalism Quarterly,* vol. 33, no. 4, pp. 423–432, 1956. Case study of gatekeeper function of sixteen wire editors concerning their criteria for inclusion or exclusion of specific wire copy. Attempts to get at perceptual and psychological correlates of these decisions. The study finds selection to be mechanistic rather than subjective.

110/ Gieber, Walter: "Do Newspapers Overplay 'Negative' News?" *Journalism Quarterly,* vol. 32, no. 3, pp. 311–318, 1955. A comparison of the news printed with that available indicates that Indiana dailies overplay negative news. The study is notable for directional categories.

111/ Gold, David, and Jerry L. Simmons: "News Selection Patterns Among Iowa Dailies," *Public Opinion Quarterly,* vol. 29, no. 3, pp. 424–430, 1965. Qualitative and quantitative analysis of inclusion of wire copy in Iowa dailies.

112/ Gregg, James E.: "Newspaper Editorial Endorsements and California Elections 1948–1962," *Journalism Quarterly,* vol. 42, no. 4, pp. 532–538, 1965. Compares eleven California newspapers with regard to editorial endorsements and election outcomes. Finds the greatest influence to be on local elections and lengthy ballots.

113/ Griggs, Harry H.: "Newspaper Performance in Recession Coverage," *Journalism Quarterly,* vol. 40, no. 4, pp. 559–564, 1963. An example of how content analysis can lead to recommendations for better news coverage. Content analysis of five newspapers for a three-month period (to study performance in recession coverage) resulted in recommendations on how to achieve better coverage of economic affairs in general and business cycles in particular.

114/ Guback, Thomas H.: "Public Issues Programs on Radio and Television, 1961," *Journalism Quarterly,* vol. 39, no. 3, pp. 373–376, 1962. Contrasts educational and commercial TV and radio in time allotted to public issues. Pilot study of cooperative research by several universities.

115/ Guttman, Louis: "An Outline of Some New Methodology for Social Research," *Public Opinion Quarterly,* vol. 18, no. 4, pp. 395–404, 1954–1955. Summarizes briefly a number of new methodological approaches that are being used at the Israel Institute of Applied Social Research. Lists publications that describe these techniques in more detail.

116/ Guttman, Louis: "A Structural Theory For Intergroup Beliefs and Action," *American Sociological Review,* vol. 24, no. 3, pp. 318–328, 1959. Suggests a structural theory (in both content and statistical form) for the observed interrelations among four subuniverses of content in connection with interracial behavior – stereotypes, norms, hypothetical interaction, and personal interaction.

117/ Hachten, William A.: "The Changing U.S. Sunday Newspaper," *Journalism Quarterly,* vol. 38, no. 3, pp. 281–288, 1961. Uses thirteen selected metropolitan Sunday papers and shows marked changes during the 1939 to 1959 period. The study is an example of sampling over a long period of time. It gives a method for avoiding bias.

118/ Hage, George S.: "Anti-Intellectualism in Press Comment: 1828 and 1952," *Journalism Quarterly,* vol. 36, no. 4, pp. 439–446, 1959. Suggests that antiintellectualism was at least as pronounced in the earlier as in the more recent campaign. Purposive sampling of newspaper titles is used, with substantive and directional categories.

119/ Hardt, Hanno, and Michael White: "Front Page News Similarity in A.M. and P.M. Papers," *Journalism Quarterly,* vol. 43, no. 3, pp. 552–555, 1966. Compares content of front pages of morning and evening papers in same community publication situations.

120/ Hart, Jim: "Election Campaign Coverage in English and U.S. Daily Newspapers," *Journalism Quarterly,* vol. 42, no. 2, pp. 213–218, 1965. Space measurement and headline classification is used in this comparative content analysis of the press coverage of two national election campaigns.

121/ Hart, Jim: "The Flow of International News into Ohio," *Journalism Quarterly,* vol. 38, no. 4, pp. 541–543, 1961. Measurement of a single category of news (foreign news). Purposive sample of dates and newspapers.

122/ Hart, Jim: "The Flow of News between the United States and Canada," *Journalism Quarterly,* vol. 40, no. 1, pp. 70–74, 1963. A quantitative study of news about the United States in four large Canadian dailies and news of Canada in four large United States dailies.

123/ Hart, Jim: "Foreign News in U.S. and English Daily Newspapers: A Comparison," *Journalism Quarterly,* vol. 43, no. 3, pp. 443–449, 1966. A comparison of the percentage of space allotted to foreign news by four United States papers and four English papers with qualitative explanations.

124/ Harvey, John: "The Content Characteristics of Best-Selling Novels," *Public Opinion Quarterly,* vol. 17, no. 1, pp. 91–114, 1953. Matches best- and poor-selling novels for theme, date of issue, length, advertising, and so on, to focus on variables of content. Concludes with sixteen variables which, in combinations of three and four, appear to provide good predictability.

125/ Haskins, J. B.: "The Editorial Mix: One Solution to a Magazine Editor's Dilemma," *Journalism Quarterly,* vol. 42, no. 4, pp. 557–562, 1965. Algorithmic analysis of item-readership data shows editors how maximum audience can be reached with a minimum of content items.

126/ Haskins, J. B.: "Headline-and-Lead Scanning vs. Whole-Item Reading in Newspaper Content Analysis," *Journalism Quarterly,* vol. 43, no. 2, pp. 333-335, 1966. Scanning only the headline and lead detected 76 per cent of newspaper items mentioning foreign affairs. The remaining 24 per cent gave only minor mention to the category. Author found headline and lead scanning satisfactory for his purposes.

127/ Haskins, J. B.: "A Simple Technique for Describing Time Trends," *Journalism Quarterly,* vol. 38, no. 1, pp. 83–84, 1961. A method of determining trend, direction, and consistency in content by using the Spearman rank-correlation method.

128/ Haskins, J.B.: "Validation of the Abstraction Index as a Tool for Content-Effects Analysis and Content Analysis," *Journal of Applied Psychology,* vol. 44, no. 2, pp. 102–110, 1960. Attempts to validate the reliability of the abstraction index as a technique for measuring readability.

129/ Hatch, Mary G., and David L. Hatch: "Problems of Married Working Women as Presented by Three Popular Working Women's Magazines," *Social Forces,* vol. 37, no. 2, pp. 148–153, 1958. Using purposive sampling of magazine titles, the study infers the attitudes of writers toward the possibility of achieving satisfactory solutions to problems.

130/ Hazard, William R., J. David Moriaty, and Victoria C. Timmons: "A Nontopical System of TV Program Categories," *Audio Visual Communication Review,* vol. 12, no. 2, pp. 146–163, 1964. Reduces television program content into a typology of topic-free, mutually exclusive categories through the use of the technique of substruction.

131/ Head, Sidney W.: "Content Analysis of Television Drama Programs," *Quarterly of Film, Radio, TV,* vol. 9, no. 2, pp. 175–194, 1954. Author reports results of a dissertation at New York University, 1952. He utilizes four content dimensions – interaction, temporal-physical, character, and behavioral. For method, the dissertation itself must be consulted, because the report in this periodical is incomplete.

132/ Hess, J. Daniel: "The Religious Journals' Image of the Mass Media," *Journalism Quarterly,* vol. 41, no. 1, pp. 106–108, 1964. Four journals are analyzed to determine the image of the mass media as portrayed by influential religious journals.

133/ Higbie, Charles E.: "Book Reviewing and Civil Rights: The

Effect of Regional Opinion," *Journalism Quarterly,* vol. 41, no. 3, pp. 385-394, 1964. A content analysis of ninety United States newspapers randomly selected. An analysis of book reviews related to civil rights indicates that practices in reviewing books differ in different regions.

134/ Higbie, Charles E. "Wisconsin Dailies in the 1952 Campaign: Space vs. Display," *Journalism Quarterly,* vol. 31, no. 1, pp. 56-60, 1954. The study is an analysis of the front pages of fourteen Wisconsin dailies during the 1952 presidential race. It analyzes headlines, pictures, and the space devoted to major political figures. The study includes exploratory analysis between type of lead in the stories and headline.

135/ Hirsch, Walter: "The Image of the Scientist in Science Fiction: A Content Analysis," *Americal Journal of Sociology,* vol. 63, no. 5, pp. 506-512, 1958. Random sample of stories published from 1926 to 1950 in science fiction magazines. Uses reliability and validity check.

136/ Holder, Harold D.: "Russian Propaganda in Exchange Publications," *Journalism Quarterly,* vol. 41, no. 3, pp. 427-429, 1964. Combines total observations for both dominant and less discussed topics of the United States in the *USSR Information Bulletin* with individual category variation.

137/ Iker, Howard P., and Norman Harway: "A Computer Approach toward the Analysis of Content," *Behavioral Science,* vol. 10, no. 2, pp. 173-182, 1965. Shows how to reduce emphasis on categorization by judges or investigators by a content analysis method developed to provide descriptions of free speech production in psychotherapeutic interviews.

138/ Inkeles, Alex, and Kent Geiger: "Critical Letters to the Editors of the Soviet Press: Areas and Modes of Complaint," *American Sociological Review,* vol. 17, no. 6, pp. 694-703, 1952. Purposive samples of letters and newspapers; arbitrary selection of time. The study has two major analytic divisions – (1) topical content and (2) characteristics of the writers and targets of criticism and the relationship of critic to criticized.

139/ Inkeles, Alex, and Kent Geiger: "Critical Letters to the Editors of the Soviet Press: Social Characteristics and Inter-Relations of Critic and Criticized," *American Sociological Review,* vol. 18, no. 1, pp. 12-22, 1953. Continuation of previous article, using different categories for analysis.

140/ Janes, Robert W.: "A Technique for Describing Community Structure through Newspaper Analysis," *Social Forces,* vol. 37, no. 2, pp. 102–109, 1958. Suggests content analysis of newspaper items to develop comparative indices of familial and associational structures of cities. Interesting methodology.

141/ Johnson, F. Craig, and George R. Klare: "General Models of Communication Research: A Survey of the Developments of a Decade," *Journal of Communication,* vol. 11, no. 1, pp. 13–26, 1961. A review of general communications models up to 1960. Models are classified as evolving from telecommunications, face-to-face communication, and general, personal communication.

142/ Jones, Robert, and Roy Carter: "Some Procedures for Estimating 'News Hole' in Content Analysis," *Public Opinion Quarterly,* vol. 23, no. 3, pp. 399-403, 1959. Establishes a constructed time period as a sampling technique to ensure equitable distribution of days over the study period. Study shows such a sampling procedure to be valid.

143/ Kaplan, Abraham: "Content Analysis and the Theory of Signs," *Philosophy of Science,* vol. 10, no. 4, pp. 230–247, 1943. A theoretical consideration of content analysis techniques and their relation to the theory of signs.

144/ Kelley, Douglas: "Press Coverage of Two Michigan Congressional Elections," *Journalism Quarterly,* vol. 35, no. 4, pp. 447–449, 1958. A study of six daily newspapers for a six-week period to discover coverage. The study is based on item count.

145/ Kent, Ruth K.: "Mental Health Coverage in Six Mass Magazines," *Journalism Quarterly,* vol. 39, no. 4, pp. 519–522, 1962. This article stresses the use of article analysis with formal rules of logic to judge the development of argumentation and structure of theories and their application to specific cases.

146/ Kerckhoff, Richard K.: "Negro News in the Daily Press: A Publicity Frame of Reference," *Social Forces,* vol. 29, no. 3, pp. 227–281, 1951. Method of sampling is not given, but the author studies Columbus, Ohio, newspapers to learn when and under what circumstances the paper's treatment of Negroes improved. A public relations expert reclassified some items, as a reliability check. Apparently there was no test to determine if differences in classifying are significant.

147/ Kerrick, Jean S., Thomas E. Anderson, and Luita B. Swales: "Balance and the Writer's Attitude in News Stories and Editorials," *Journalism Quarterly,* vol. 41, no. 2, pp. 207–215, 1964. An experimental study involving students writing news stories and editorials with attitude, editorial policy, and bias as independent variables. Chi-square and randomization tests.

148/ Kish, Leslie: "Sampling Organizations and Groups of Unequal Sizes," *American Sociological Review,* vol. 30, no. 4, pp. 564–572, 1965. An excellent consideration of the effect of the unit characteristic on individual elements. Particular emphasis is placed on possible mistaken assignments of observation units.

149/ Klapper, Joseph T.: "Studying Effects of Mass Communication," *Teachers College Record,* vol. 57, no. 2, pp. 95–103, 1955. A recent reevaluation of content analysis procedures suggests new and broader principles and bases for this study. Points out that content is only one element in the complex of effects. [See also Joseph Klapper, *Effects of Mass Communications* (New York: The Free Press of Glencoe), 1960].

150/ Klein, Malcolm, and Nathan Maccoby: "Newspaper Objectivity in the 1952 Campaign," *Journalism Quarterly,* vol. 31, no. 3, pp. 285–296, 1954. Usefulness of quantitative methods in judging newspaper bias is demonstrated. Indices of objectivity are developed for a sample of eight prominent United States dailies.

151/ Kobre, Sidney: "How Florida Dailies Handled the 1952 Presidential Campaign," *Journalism Quarterly,* vol. 30, no. 2, pp. 163–169, 1953. Content analyzed for emphasis on the basis of eight criteria (including items, headline, length, page, position on page, and pictures).

152/ Kobre, Sidney, and Juanita Parks: "The Newspapers Cover a Murder Case," *Journalism Quarterly,* vol. 31, no. 3, pp. 311–318, 1954. Using qualitative analysis, the study tries to determine how newspapers cover crimes committed by the mentally ill.

153/ Kracauer, Siegfried: "The Challenge of Qualitative Analysis," *Public Opinion Quarterly,* vol. 16, no. 4, pp. 631–641, 1952. Challenges techniques of quantitative analysis as unreliable. States an approach that frankly admits the impressionistic part of analysis as a factor and tries to control it through a disciplined subjectivity.

154/ Krieghbaum, Hillier: "Two Gemini Space Flights in Two Metropolitan Dailies," *Journalism Quarterly,* vol. 43, no. 1, pp. 120–121, 1966. Comparison of coverage of the flight of Gemini-4 and Gemini-5 by *The New York Times* and the New York *Post.*

155/ Kriesberg, Martin: "Soviet News in the *'New York Times',*" *Public Opinion Quarterly,* vol. 10, no. 4, pp. 540–564, 1946. An early attempt at devising an attention score based on placement of items.

156/ Lambert, Verdelle: "Negro Exposure in *Look's* Editorial Content," *Journalism Quarterly*, vol. 42, no. 4, pp. 657–659, 1965. Content analysis compares two one-year periods, 1959–1960 and 1963–1964, as to the amount of inclusion of reference to the Negro in both editorial and pictorial sections.

157/ Landis, Jack B.: "Multiple Regression Analysis – the Easy Way," *Journal of Advertising Research*, vol. 2, no. 1, pp. 35–42, 1962. A step-by-step iteration and explanation of how media researchers use this technique. It shows a typical problem and includes possible shortcuts and spots to be double checked.

158/ Lee, John: "International News Flow in the Expatriate English-Language Press," *Journalism Quarterly*, vol. 42, no. 4, pp. 632–638, 1965. Analysis of sources of news for English-language newspapers in foreign countries.

159/ Lerner, Daniel, Ithiel deSola Pool, and Harold Lasswell: "Comparative Analysis of Political Ideologies: A Preliminary Statement," *Public Opinion Quarterly*, vol. 15, no. 4, pp. 713–733, 1951. Content analysis to assess "the world revolution of our time." Authors compile a list of symbols and words dealing with political ideologies. They tabulate symbols and make judgments of directions.

160/ Levine, Edward P.: "Studying the American Press: The Walter Jenkins Case," *Journalism Quarterly*, vol. 43, no. 3, pp. 493–496, 1966. Levine studies uniformity and fairness of the press in coverage of this story and identifies and analyzes with respect to nature of AP and UPI wire copy.

161/ Lewin, Kurt: "Frontiers in Group Dynamics. II, Channels of Group Life; Social Planning and Action Research," *Human Relations*, vol. 1, no. 2, pp. 143–153, 1947. A simple, illustrated discussion of Lewin's gatekeeping concept appears in this article.

162/ Lewis, Howard: "The Cuban Revolt Story: AP, UPI and Three Papers," *Journalism Quarterly*, vol. 37, no. 4, pp. 573–578, 1960. An analysis of the Castro revolt and newspaper coverage of it. A one-month study of AP and UPI stories and their use or nonuse by three leading United States dailies.

163/ Liebes, B. H.: "Decision-Making by Telegraph Editors – AP or UPI?" *Journalism Quarterly*, vol. 43, no. 3, pp. 334–342, 1966. Gatekeeper study comparing AP and UPI.

164/ Loftus, Beverly: "Ezra Pound and the Bollingen Prize: The Controversy in Periodicals," *Journalism Quarterly,* vol. 39, no. 3, pp. 347–354, 1962. Twenty periodicals are studied for anti- and pro-Pound content.

165/ Lyle, Jack, and Walter Wilcox: "Television News – An Interim Report," *Journal of Broadcasting,* vol. 7, no. 2, pp. 157–166, 1963. Studies news stories in Los Angeles dailies and on local TV stations to compare media. Includes interviews with news executives on policies.

166/ Lynch, Mervin D., and Atiyz Effendi: "Editorial Treatment of India in the New York *Times,*" *Journalism Quarterly,* vol. 41, no. 3, pp. 430–432, 1964. Evaluative-assertion analysis, as developed by Charles E. Osgood and modified by Bruce H. Westley, is used to provide an assessment of the treatment of India in the editorial columns of *The New York Times.*

167/ Maccoby, Nathan, Freddie O. Sabghir, and Bryant Cushing: "A Method for the Analysis of the News Coverage of Industry," *Public Opinion Quarterly,* vol. 14, no. 4, pp. 751–758, 1950. Uses content categories and direction categories, but does not tell how evaluations were made.

168/ MacLean, Malcolm S., Jr.: "Some Multivariate Designs for Communications Research," *Journalism Quarterly,* vol. 42, no. 4, pp. 614–622, 1965. Discusses several analytic models of factor analysis illustrating some actual uses and possible applications of the techniques in communication research.

169/ Markham, James W.: "Foreign News in the United States and South American Press," *Public Opinion Quarterly,* vol. 25, no. 2, pp. 249–262, 1961. Uses purposive sampling on basis of circulation size, geographical distribution, and prestige. Table of random numbers is used to draw sample of thirty days from three-month period. Classifies news by subject and world areas.

170/ Markham, James W.: "Press Treatment of the 1958 State Elections in Pennsylvania," *The Western Political Quarterly,* vol. 14, no. 4, pp. 912–924, 1961. Estimates of performance are based on six dimensions of news coverage: news-story content (volume and direction), mention of issues (frequency and direction), headlines (frequency and direction), illustrations (size and referent), front-page story content, and front-page headline treatment. Twenty-six newspapers were studied over a one-month period.

171/ Markham, James W., and Guido H. Stempel III, "Analysis of Techniques in Measuring Press Performance," *Journalism Quarterly,* vol. 34, no. 2, pp. 187–190, 1957. Study of twenty-four Pennsylvania dailies during October, 1956, finds that space measurements can be used alone as a research technique, disregarding headline-size analysis and counting of mentions of themes or issues in the news.

172/ Martin, L. John, and Harold L. Nelson, "The Historical Standard in Analyzing Press Performance," *Journalism Quarterly,* vol. 33, no. 4, pp. 456–466, 1956. Discusses the problems of constructing a historical standard against which a periodical's performance in reporting events can be analyzed. An expansion of Berelson's work.

173/ Maynard, Edwin H.: "An Analysis of Church Magazine Editorials," *Journalism Quarterly,* vol. 33, no. 3, p. 367, 1956. Qualitative analysis of 138 editorials published in twelve denominational magazines.

174/ McAllister, William H. III: "The Effects of Bylines on News Story Credibility," *Journalism Quarterly,* vol. 43, no. 2, pp. 331–332, 1966. Qualitative and quantitative effects of the use of the byline.

175/ McDowell, James L.: "The Role of Newspapers in Illinois' At-Large Election," *Journalism Quarterly,* vol. 42, no. 2, pp. 281–284, 1965. The educational and guidance functions of fifteen Illinois daily newspapers are examined during the 1964 Illinois state House of Representatives election. A comparison of election results with newspapers' support of candidates shows that newspapers making specific recommendations to readers had a significant influence on the election outcome. Caution must be stressed when trying to determine the relative effect of endorsements because of so many other variables.

176/ McQuitty, Louis L.: "Elementary Linkage Analysis For Isolating Orthogonal and Oblique Types and Typal Relevancies," *Educational and Psychological Measurement,* vol. 17, no. 2, pp. 207–229, 1957. Develops and illustrates a rapid and objective method for clustering variables into types, with suggestions for extending the method.

177/ Merrill, John C.: "How *Time* Stereotyped Three U.S. Presidents," *Journalism Quarterly,* vol. 42, no. 4, pp. 563–570, 1965. Discussion of sterotyped images of three Presidents – Truman, Eisenhower, and Kennedy – as presented by *Time.* The article includes an analysis of techniques used.

178/ Merrill, John C.: "The Image of the United States in Ten Mexican

Dailies," *Journalism Quarterly,* vol. 39, no. 2, pp. 203–209, 1962. Content analysis employing a variety of content categories for United States news in the Mexican press. Serves as an excellent example of an image study. Uses purposive sample of titles, measurement of column inches, and thematic analysis.

179/ Merrill, John C.: "The Image of the 'Yanqui' in the Mexican Press," *Gazette,* vol. 8, no. 3, pp. 251–254, 1962. Ten Mexican dailies are examined for amount and type of United States news. Images and themes are constructed.

180/ Merritt, Richard L.: "Public Opinion in Colonial America: Content Analyzing the Colonial Press," *Public Opinion Quarterly,* vol. 27, no. 3, pp. 356–371, 1963. Choosing an appropriate time span and sample size and other experiences of the author in content analyzing the colonial press have application for present research on a more advanced level in time press.

181/ Middleton, Russell: "Fertility Values in American Magazine Fiction, 1916–1956," *Public Opinion Quarterly,* vol. 24, no. 1, pp. 139–143, 1960. The changing size of families in short stories is seen as an index to changing values and parallels actual fertility rates.

182/ Mullen, James J.: "How Candidates for the Senate Use Newspaper Advertising," *Journalism Quarterly,* vol. 40, no. 4, pp. 533–538, 1963. A content analysis of newspaper advertising for candidates in sixteen races for the United States Senate.

183/ Mullen, James J.: "Newspaper Advertising in the Kennedy-Nixon Campaign," *Journalism Quarterly,* vol. 40, no. 1, pp. 3-11, 1963. All the advertisements for presidential candidates in a sample of eighty newspapers are analyzed for content during the fourteen days immediately preceding the election (October 25 to November 7).

184/ Nasir, Sari J.: "The Arab World in U.S. Movie Titles," *Journalism Quarterly,* vol. 40, no. 3, pp. 351–353, 1963. Sixty-four years of movie titles are examined for references to the world of the Arabs. A latent structure analysis.

185/ Nasir, Sari J.: "The Portrayal of the Arab World in Men's Popular Magazines," *Journal of Human Relations,* vol. 12, no. 3, pp. 424–435, 1964. An analysis of the themes, characters, and settings of the stories found in popular magazines for men indicates that the "Arabian Nights" stereotypes of the Arab world still exist, at least in men's magazines.

186/ Newman, Sidney H.: "Quantitative Analysis of Verbal Evaluations," *Journal of Applied Psychology,* vol. 38, no. 5, pp. 293–296, 1954. The article describes the development and reliability of a procedure for scoring comments obtained from an efficiency report.

187/ Nixon, Raymond, and Robert L. Jones: "The Content of Non-Competitive vs. Competitive Newspapers," *Journalism Quarterly,* vol. 33, no. 3, pp. 299–314, 1956. A content analysis of matched pairs of dailies based on news hole analysis. It includes extensive categorization by subject.

188/ Nord, Bruce A.: "Press Freedom and Political Structure," *Journalism Quarterly,* vol. 43, no. 3, pp. 531–534, 1966. Content analysis provides the basis for classifying press freedom in Ghana and Nigeria.

189/ Oliphant, C. A.: "The Image of the United States Projected by *Peking Review,*" *Journalism Quarterly,* vol. 41, no. 3, pp. 416–420, 1964. Less of a content analysis than a selection of themes recurring in one publication. The themes are used to illustrate the Chinese Communist attitudes and opinions of the United States projected by that publication.

190/ Orr, David B.: "The Evaluation of Televised Instruction," *Audio Visual Communication Review,* vol. 14, no. 3, pp. 363–370, 1966. Content analysis of programming of WQED compared to predetermined objectives.

191/ Osgood, Charles E., Sol Saporta, and Jum C. Nunnally: "Evaluative Assertion Analysis," *Littera,* vol. 3, pp. 47–102, 1956. Development of the technique of evaluative-assertion analysis, which minimizes the bias of the analyst. Evaluative scaling of attitude objects referred to by the source.

192/ Osgood, Charles E., and Evelyn B. Walker, "Motivation and Language Behavior: A Content Analysis of Suicide Notes," *Journal of Abnormal and Social Psychology,* vol. 59, no. 1, pp. 58–67, 1959. A content analysis of real and fake suicide notes and ordinary letters reveals suicide notes displayed greater stereotyping in writing. The study may be helpful as a reference in symbol analysis and for use in developing indices for measuring conflict in news.

193/ Otto, Herbert A.: "Sex and Violence on the American Newsstand," *Journalism Quarterly,* vol. 40, no. 1, pp. 19–26, 1963. Actually three research projects over a two-year period, this study includes content analyses of fifty-five magazines and the covers of 296 paperback books available on newsstands, plus an analysis of ten leading United States newspapers. The care taken to maintain thorough comprehension of counting procedures and uniformity in analysis are good guides for all content analyses.

194/ Papageorgis, Demetrios: "Prevention and Treatment in Mental Health Communications," *Public Opinion Quarterly,* vol. 19, no. 1, pp. 107–119, 1965. Analysis of content of existing communication about mental health. Compares messages emphasizing treatment with those stressing prevention.

195/ Peterson, Wilbur, and Robert Thorp: "Weeklies' Editorial Effort Less than 30 Years Ago," *Journalism Quarterly,* vol. 39, no. 1, pp. 53–56, 1962. A sample of 215 of Iowa's non-daily newspapers shows amount of editorial effort in four circulation classes. It classifies editorials by subject, length, and position. An expanded version of this article appeared in *The Iowa Publisher,* March, 1962.

196/ Powers, Richard D.: "Sampling Problems in Studies of Writing Style," *Journal of Applied Psychology,* vol. 38, no. 2, pp. 105–108, 1954. This study demonstrates the use of cluster sampling of sentences to test differences in writing style. It is especially helpful for content analyses using key words or themes.

197/ Price, Granville: "A Method for Analyzing Newspaper Campaign Coverage," *Journalism Quarterly,* vol. 31, no. 4, pp. 447–458, 1954. Outlines plan for measuring intensity of a newspaper's political leanings in several areas of news performance using simple statistical concepts.

198/ Rarick Galen, and Hartman Barrie: "The Effects of Competition on One Daily Newspaper's Content," *Journalism Quarterly,* vol. 43, no. 3, pp. 459–469, 1966. This analysis of a single newspaper in periods of no, moderate, and intense competition indicates that as competition pressure increases, choice of local and immediate reward items increases.

199/ Rosi, Eugene J.: "How 50 Periodicals and the *Times* Interpreted the Test Ban Controversy," *Journalism Quarterly,* vol. 41, no. 4, pp. 545–556, 1964. *The New York Times* editorials and articles published in various publications are examined to determine what mass communications elites contributed to the debate on the barring of nuclear-weapons.

200/ Rothman, Robert A., and Donald W. Olmsted: "Chicago *Tribune* Cartoons During and After the McCormick Era," *Journalism Quarterly,* vol. 43, no. 1, pp. 67–72, 1966. This content analysis shows that most cartoons concerned political matters, were generally national in scope, and referred to perennial political issues. Use of symbolic figures was greater than use of actual persons, and portrayals of actual people were mostly negative.

201/ Rowse, Arthur E.: "Measuring for Bias," *American Editor,* vol. 1, no. 4, p. 22, 1958. The author states that space measurement to learn fairness of political news should be subordinated to subjective judgments of a panel of newsmen.

202/ Rucker, Bryce W.: "News Services, Crowd Reporting in the 1956 Presidential Campaign," *Journalism Quarterly,* vol. 37, no. 2, pp. 195–198, 1960. Thirty judges rated the favorableness to candidates of descriptions of crowd reaction that appeared in wire-service stories. The Associated Press, United Press, and International News Service differed in their reports of reactions to candidates, their overall attention to crowd reports, and their estimates of crowd size.

203/ Sander, Luther W.: "A Content Analysis of President Kennedy's First Six Press Conferences," *Journalism Quarterly,* vol. 42, no. 1, pp. 114–115, 1965. Audio tape recordings are used as basic source material for this descriptive content analysis of John F. Kennedy's first six press conferences as the nation's leader.

204/ Schillinger, Elisabeth Hupp: "British and U.S. Newspaper Coverage of the Bolshevik Revolution," *Journalism Quarterly,* vol. 43, no. 1, pp. 10–17, 1966. An analysis and comparison of news coverage and editorial comment at the time of the November, 1917, revolution, as found in the *London Times, Manchester Guardian, New York Times,* and *Chicago Tribune,* finds the coverage lacking in accuracy, depth, and objectivity. Reasons: ". . . reliable sources were difficult to locate, compromises were made, and rumors took the place of fact."

205/ Schramm, Wilbur: "Newspapers of a State as a News Network," *Journalism Quarterly,* vol. 35, no. 2, pp. 177–182, 1958. Studies news content of all Oregon dailies for one week. Simply counts the news items in each newspaper and records the source of each item.

206/ Schutz, William C.: "On Categorizing Qualitative Data in Content Analysis," *Public Opinion Quarterly,* vol. 22, no. 4, pp. 503-515, 1958. This paper analyzes the problem of judging qualitative data and proposes a method for coping with it.

207/ Schuneman, R. Smith: "Visual Aspects of T.V. News: Communicator, Message, Equipment," *Journalism Quarterly,* vol. 43, no. 2, pp. 281–286, 1966. The visual aspects of newscasts are given a cursory analysis.

208/ Scott, William A.: "Reliability of Content Analysis: The Case of Nominal Scale Coding," *Public Opinion Quarterly,* vol. 19, no. 3, pp. 321–325, 1955. It offers a measure for reliability and an index for intercoder agreement, which are applicable to content analysis. Use of the index requires some statistical knowledge.

209/ Sebald, Hans: "Studying National Character Through Comparative Content Analysis," *Social Forces,* vol. 40, no. 4, pp. 318–322, 1962. The prevailing values in a German (Nazi) song book subordinated the individual to the authority of the larger social system and lauded heroic death. An American song book of the same year (1940) did neither.

210/ Shanor, Donald R.: "The New York Columnists Look At Lindsay," *Journalism Quarterly,* vol. 43, no. 2, pp. 287–290, 1966. Analysis of the editorial position of the New York *Times, Herald Tribune, News, World-Telegram and Sun, Post,* and *Journal-American* toward John Lindsay.

211/ Shepard, David W.: "Henry J. Taylor's Radio Talks: A Content Analysis," *Journalism Quarterly,* vol. 33, no. 1, pp. 15–22, 1956. A content analysis of broadcast content, it establishes reliability of method and counts assertions.

212/ Sherburne, E. G., Jr.: "Science on Television: A Challenge to Creativity," *Journalism Quarterly,* vol. 40, no. 3, pp. 300–305, 1963. Analyzes one day's network shows for scientific content using a broad definition of science.

213/ Sherif, Carolyn W., and Norman R. Jackman: "Judgments of Truth by Participants in Collective Controversy," *Public Opinion Quarterly,* vol. 15, no. 2, pp. 173–186, 1966. This study uses the Oklahoma battle over prohibition repeal in 1959 to investigate the ways in which participants assess the truth of conflicting statements of fact. Statements were arrived at in part through content analysis.

214/ Simmons, George E.: "The Communist Conspiracy Case: Views of 72 Daily Newspapers," *Journalism Quarterly,* vol. 27, no. 1, pp. 3–11, 1950. An impressionistic study, it is an analysis of content without quantitative units.

215/ Smith, James Steel: "America's Magazine Missionaries of Culture," *Journalism Quarterly,* vol. 43, no. 3, pp. 449–459, 1966. A handful of magazines have promoted culture. This study of their life spans show they have a pattern of rise and then fall.

216/ Sorensen, Robert C., and Theodore C. Sorenson: "A Proposal for the Use of Content Analysis in Literary Infringement Cases," *Social Forces,* vol. 33, no. 3, pp. 262–267, 1955. Content analysis makes it possible to isolate, classify, and inventory quantitatively the words and themes in a piece of literature. This presents a statistical opportunity to figure the probabilities that similarity between two articles, for example, did not occur by chance.

217/ Spiegelman, M., C. Terwilliger, and F. Fearing: "A Content Analysis of Sunday Comic Strips: A Study in a Mass Medium of Communication," *Journal of Social Psychology,* vol. 35, no. 1, pp. 35–37, 1952. This study demonstrates the use of content analysis in psychological research.

218/ Startt, James D.: "Early Press Reaction to Wilson's League Proposal," *Journalism Quarterly,* vol. 39, no. 1, pp. 301–308, 1962. This impressionistic study examines press opinion of the League of Nations and the doubts and opposition that led to Wilson's defeat.

219/ Steigleman, Walter: "Range and Quality of High School Editorials," *Journalism Quarterly,* vol. 39, no. 1, pp. 92–94, 1962. Six major categories are used with thematic classification based on dominant themes to study 714 editorials submitted in the annual writers' contest of *Quill and Scroll.*

220/ Stempel, Guido H., III: "Content Patterns of Small and Metropolitan Dailies," *Journalism Quarterly,* vol. 39, no. 1, pp. 88–90, 1962. This study points out similarities in the percentages of space allotted various types of news in two classes of dailies.

221/ Stempel, Guido H., III: "How Newspapers Use the Associated Press Afternoon A-Wire," *Journalism Quarterly,* vol. 41, no. 3, pp. 380–384, 1964. Studies how AP items are used by twenty dailies and relates this to time items. The author studied all editions for one week and made item and headline type counts.

222/ Stempel, Guido H., III: "Increasing Reliability in Content Analysis," *Journalism Quarterly,* vol. 32, no. 4, pp. 449–455, 1955. Points out the need for concern about reliability in content analysis and the ways in which reliability errors can be reduced.

223/ Stempel, Guido H., III: "The Prestige Press Covers the 1960 Presidential Campaign," *Journalism Quarterly,* vol. 38, no. 2, pp. 157–163, 1961. Using two analysis techniques–space measurement and headline classification–the author found that fifteen dailies rated by editors as superior in news coverage and integrity gave, as a group, virtually equal amounts of space in their news columns to Democratic and Republican campaigns.

224/ Stempel, Guido H., III: "The Prestige Press in Two Presidential Elections," *Journalism Quarterly,* vol. 42, no. 1, pp. 15–21, 1965. Space measurement and headline classification are the main means used to study fifteen leading dailies and their performance in the 1960 and 1964 presidential elections.

225/ Stempel, Guido H., III: "Sample Size for Classifying Subject Matter in Dailies," *Journalism Quarterly,* vol. 29, no. 3, pp. 333–334, 1952. Establishes the validity of varying sample sizes for use in classifying daily newspaper content.

226/ Stempel, Guido H., III: "Uniformity of Wire Content of Six Michigan Dailies," *Journalism Quarterly,* vol. 36, no. 1, pp. 45–48, 1959. This study of a week's content of six small dailies gives examples of subject categories.

227/ Stene, E. O.: "Newspapers in the Campaign," *Social Science,* vol. 12, no. 2, pp. 213–215, 1937. Objective method of determining differences in newspapers' coverage of election news.

228/ Stephenson, William: "A Critique of Content Analysis," *The Psychological Record,* vol. 13, no. 2, pp. 155–162, 1963. A critique based on the assumption that content analysis has no theoretical base. The study indicates ways in which the necessary theoretical base could be provided for sound theoretical use of content analysis.

229/ Stephenson, William: "The 'Infantile' vs. the 'Sublime' in Advertisements," *Journalism Quarterly,* vol. 40, no. 2, pp. 181–186, 1963 This trend analysis uses categories of mechanisms operating in advertisements. *Q* sorts are subjected to variance and factor analyses. Chi square.

230/ Stern, Bernard: "How Local Governmental News is Handled by Three Dailies," *Journalism Quarterly,* vol. 27, no. 2, pp. 149–156, 1950. The author employs three techniques: item count, space count, and readability study.

231/ Stevenson, Robert L.: "Readability of Conservative and Sensational Papers since 1872," *Journalism Quarterly,* vol. 41, no. 2, pp. 201–206, 1964. Six United States dailies are examined with the revised Flesch formula, using a random and nonrandom sampling of issues and items since 1872. T tests are made for the significance of means.

232/ Stewart, Janice S.: "Content and Readership of Teen Magazines," *Journalism Quarterly,* vol. 41, no. 4, pp. 580–583, 1964. A content analysis is used to provide a descriptive overview of the magazines aimed at the thirteen-to-nineteen age group. A questionnaire is also used to measure the importance and the influence of the publications for teenage readers.

233/ Stone, Philip F., et al.: "The General Inquirer: A Computer System for Content Analysis and Retrieval Based on the Sentence as a Unit of Information," *Behavioral Science*, vol. 7, no. 4, pp. 484–498, 1962. This article describes the COMIT program. The authors developed an analysis of various verbal reports for the IBM 7090 computer so that others could construct dictionaries, sentence-editing rules, and other necessary material.

234/ Stoodley, Bartlett: "Bias in Reporting the FCC Investigation," *Public Opinion Quarterly*, vol. 24, no. 1, pp. 92–98, 1960. The study shows that a Democratic newspaper gave more emphasis to stories about the House investigation of the Federal Communications Commission (in terms of headlines, column inches, choice of language, and other means) than did a Republican newspaper.

235/ Tannenbaum, Percy H.: "The Indexing Process in Communication," *Public Opinion Quarterly*, vol. 19, no. 3, pp. 292–302, 1955. An attempt to broaden the units of content analysis in order to meet wider criteria of what is communicated.

236/ Tannenbaum, Percy H., and Richard K. Brewer: "Consistency of Syntactic Structure as a Factor in Journalistic Style," *Journalism Quarterly*, vol. 42, no. 2, pp. 273–275, 1965. The authors study wire copy and alter experimental word set to determine role of syntax in news style.

237/ Tannenbaum, Percy H., and Mervin D. Lynch: "Sensationalism: The Concept and Its Measurement," *Journalism Quarterly*, vol. 37, no. 3, pp. 381–392, 1960. Uses an empirical approach to identify the dimensions of the judgment of sensationalism; develops a semantic-differential index of the sensationalism of messages. Describes the "sendex" technique and its use. Includes factor analysis.

238/ Tannenbaum, Percy H., and Mervin D. Lynch: "Sensationalism: Some Objective Message Correlates," *Journalism Quarterly*, vol. 39, no. 3, pp. 317–323, 1962. A description of efforts to isolate and identify some objectively determined message characteristics for the study of sensationalistic journalism.

239/ Tannenbaum, Percy H., and James E. Noah: "Sportugese: A Study of Sports Page Communication," *Journalism Quarterly*, vol. 36, no. 2, pp. 163–170, 1959. An analysis of agreement among sports writers on specific symbols.

240/ Taylor, Wilson L.: " 'Cloze Procedure': A New Tool for Measuring Readability," *Journalism Quarterly,* vol. 30, no. 4, pp. 415–433, 1953. Develops a method of determining effectiveness of communication in terms of reading ease. The method compares favorably with Flesch and Dale-Chall devices for measuring readability.

241/ Taylor, Wilson L.: "Gauging the Mental Health Content of the Mass Media," *Journalism Quarterly,* vol. 34, no. 2, pp. 191–201, 1957. Factor analysis is used to develop a natural set of content categories for mental-health statements in the mass media.

242/ Tichenor, Phillip: "Newspaper Usage of County Agents' Personal News Columns," *Journalism Quarterly,* vol. 36, no. 3, pp. 354-356, 1959. An analysis of news columns written by county agents for weeklies and small dailies. Simple counting, using measures of percentage of potential use; regularity of use, reading ease, and human interest (Flesch); timeliness of information; subject matter (twelve categories).

243/ Trenchard, Kendall, and W. J. E. Crissy: "Readability of Advertising and Editorial Copy in *Time* and *Newsweek,*" *Journal of Applied Psychology,* vol. 36, no. 3, pp. 161–163, 1952. A trend analysis studying the differences in reading ease in advertising and editorial copy for two five-year periods—1936–1940 and 1945-1949.

244/ Troldahl, Verling C.: "Studies of Consumption of Mass Media Content," *Journalism Quarterly,* vol. 42, no. 4, pp. 596–605, 1965. An analysis of the meaning elicited by content. Discusses various techniques of measurement for the quantitative and qualitative aspects of content.

245/ Unger, Aryah L.: "The Public Opinion Reports of the Nazi Party," *Public Opinion Quarterly,* vol. 29, no. 4, pp. 565–582, 1966. Captured archives of the Third Reich offer some insight into the manner in which the Nazi party discharged its public-opinion function. This article is an examination of the scope and quality of the Nazi party's reporting system, based mainly on the reports of local and regional party functionaries and partly on a comparison of these reports with similar materials and records of Nazi security agencies.

246/ Van Horn, George: "Analysis of AP News of Trunk and Wisconsin State Wires," *Journalism Quarterly,* vol. 29, no. 4, pp. 426–432, 1952. Extends subject categories of news content.

247/ Waltzer, Herbert: "In the Magic Lantern: T.V. Coverage of the 1964 National Conventions," *Public Opinion Quarterly,* vol. 30, no. 1, pp. 33–54, 1966. This review of the TV coverage of national party conventions raises questions and points up problems that will be relevant in elections.

248/ Wayne, Ivor: "American and Soviet Themes and Values: A Content Analysis of Pictures in Popular Magazines," *Public Opinion Quarterly*, vol. 20, no. 1, pp. 314–320, 1956. An analysis of picture content employing categories of expressed themes. It is one of the few studies devoted to the analysis of photographs and should be useful for most general content analyses.

249/ Weingast, David E.: "Walter Lippmann: A Content Analysis," *Public Opinion Quarterly*, vol. 14, no. 2, pp. 296–302, 1950. New Deal issues are used as content categories. The author evaluates Lippmann's view as favorable, unfavorable, or neutral and tabulates only those references in which Lippmann expressed a value judgment.

250/ Westley, Bruce H., Charles Higbie, et al.: "The News Magazines and the 1960 Conventions," *Journalism Quarterly*, vol. 40, no. 4, pp. 525–531, 1963. Bias in the three leading news magazines is explored by evaluative assertion analysis, combining the potency and activity dimensions into Osgood's dynamism dimension. Measures proportion of positive assertions.

251/ Westley, Bruce H., and Malcolm S. MacLean, Jr.: "A Conceptual Model for Communications Research," *Journalism Quarterly*, vol. 34, no. 1, pp. 31–38, 1957. This model places emphasis on the role of communicator and is perhaps the most useful yet developed in our field.

252/ White, David Manning: "The 'Gate Keeper': A Case Study in the Selection of News," *Journalism Quarterly*, vol. 27, no. 4, pp. 383–390, 1950. This field study quantitatively and qualitatively analyzes a typical wire editor's decisions for inclusion and exclusion of wire-copy articles. A basis for more generalized hypotheses about the gatekeeper function.

253/ Wilcox, Walter: "The Press of the Radical Right: An Exploratory Analysis," *Journalism Quarterly*, vol. 39, no. 2, pp. 152–160, 1962. The author seeks to establish a method for defining and identifying the radical-right press, as distinguished from the ultraconservative press. He reports on an intensive study of the themes of two bellwether radical-right publications, *Common Sense* and *The Cross and the Flag*. He employs a semantic measure with assigned scale values.

254/ Wilensky, Harold L.: "Mass Society and Mass Culture: Interdependence or Independence?" *American Sociological Review,* vol. 25, no. 2, pp. 173–197, 1964. Uses fixed esthetic standards, pooled judgments, and expert classification to separate media offerings into highbrow and lowbrow categories to determine level of media exposure and level of culture.

255/ Winick, Charles: "Trends in the Occupations of Celebrities: A Study of Newsmagazine Profiles and Television Interviews," *Journal of Social Psychology,* vol. 60, no. 2, pp. 301–310, 1963. Content analysis applied to print and electronic media.

256/ Wolfe, Wayne: "Images of the United States in the Latin American Press," *Journalism Quarterly,* vol. 41, no. 1, pp. 79–86, 1964. A content analysis of twenty leading morning dailies in capital cities of Latin America finds twelve clear images of the United States.

257/ Zuegner, Charles W.: "A Study of Political News in Two Major Dailies," *Journalism Quarterly,* vol. 33, no. 2, pp. 222–224, 1956. A qualitative content analysis determines how two newspapers covered the first one hundred days of President Eisenhower. Author terms analysis both quantitative and qualitative, but gives no evidence of quantification.

PAPERS AND MONOGRAPHS

258/ Adams, John B.: "Content Analyzing Wire Service Copy," paper presented at the Association for Education in Journalism (A.E.J.) convention, Austin, Texas, 1964. It describes a project involving computer use in content analysis.

259/ Adams, John B.: "The Foreign Correspondent and His Readers," paper presented at the A.E.J. convention, Syracuse, New York, 1965. A good illustration of hypothesis testing in content analysis.

260/ Caldwell, William S.: "Selected Bibliography on Propaganda Analysis, Content and Themes," Department of Journalism, University of California at Los Angeles, 1962. A bibliography of twenty-eight entries, each of which is briefly annotated.

261/ Danielson, Wayne A.: "Applying Guttman Scaling to Content Analysis," paper presented at the A.E.J. convention, Ann Arbor, Michigan, 1961. It applies Guttman scales to newspaper content analysis and to completeness of coverage in the 1960 presidential election, using twelve criterion newspapers. It gives examples and suggestions for future applications.

262/ Danielson, Wayne A., and Harold L. Jackson, "Magnetic Tape Context Scanner Program," *Programming Note 98*, Computation Center, University of North Carolina, Chapel Hill, N.C., 1963. Program for identifying designated content symbols and providing printout of designated unit and surrounding context.

263/ Gerbner, George: "Mass Communications and Popular Conceptions of Education; A Cross-Cultural Study," Institute of Communication Research, University of Illinois, Urbana, Ill., 1964. Uses wide range of content analysis techniques to gather data for this massive report.

264/ Harrison, Randall, and Malcolm S. MacLean, Jr.: "Facets of Facial Communication," School of Journalism, University of Iowa, Iowa City, Iowa, 1965. This is a clear example of the use of factor analysis techniques.

265/ Hass, Michael: "Thematic Content Analysis in the Study of Diplomatic Documents," *Studies in International Conflict and Integration*, Stanford University Press, Stanford, Calif., 1961. A thorough discussion of coding and related procedures.

266/ Hays, D. G.: "Automatic Content Analysis: Some Entries for a Transformation Catalogue," The RAND Corporation, Santa Monica, Calif., 1962. Explores the adaptability of a sentence-structure determinator or parsing routine, a routine for linguistic simplification, and a routine for transformation from linguistic to sociological variables to an automatic content analysis.

267/ Hazard, William R.: "Substruction in Content Analysis: A Non-Topical Reduction of Property Space," University of Texas, Austin, Tex., 1963. It includes six topic-free categories for content analysis of television programs.

268/ MacLean, Malcolm S., Jr.: "Some Multivariate Designs for Communication Research," paper presented at the A.E.J. convention, Syracuse, New York, 1965. Extends presentation of material in a *Journalism Quarterly* article [see (168)].

269/ MacLean, Malcolm S., Jr.: "Systems of News Communication," paper presented to the first International Symposium on Communication Theory and Research, Excelsior Springs, Missouri, 1965, School of Journalism, University of Iowa, Iowa City, Iowa.

270/ Nelson, Jerome L., and Alex S. Edelstein: "Some Inferences from a General System of Categories for the Classification of Cartoon Humor," paper presented at the A.E.J. convention, Syracuse, New York, 1965. Report by the authors on progress in developing a system of categories for analyzing a specific type of content.

271/ Pool, Ithiel deSola: *The 'Prestige Papers': A Survey of Their Editorials* (Stanford, Calif.: Stanford University Press), 1952. This is a good example of symbol analysis over time (trend analysis) and across national boundaries. It includes considerable data on the editors of the various newspapers studied.

272/ Pool, Ithiel deSola: *Symbols of Democracy* (Stanford, Calif.: Stanford University Press), 1952. This symbol analysis show trends in the attention the prestige newspapers paid to fifty-seven key terms relating to democracy (including such negative symbols as "authoritarian").

273/ Pool, Ithiel deSola: *Symbols of Internationalism* (Stanford, Calif: Stanford University Press), 1951. This is another in the series of symbol studies authored by Pool.

274/ Shaw, Donald L.: "News Bias and the Telegraph," paper presented at the A.E.J. convention, Iowa City, Iowa, 1966. Methodologically interesting for applying content analysis to historical research, determining an operational definition of news bias, studying a random sample using a modified constructed week, and relating decline in bias to increase in use of wire news. Based on Shaw's unpublished doctoral dissertation, "Bias in the News," University of Wisconsin, Madison, Wis., 1966.

275/ Stempel, Guido H., III: "Content Patterns in Presidential Campaign Coverage," paper presented at the A.E.J. convention, Syracuse, New York, 1965. An example of the use of McQuitty's elementary linkage analysis.

276/ Sutton, Willis A., Jr., and Jerry Russell: "The Social Dimensions of Kentucky Counties," Bureau of Community Service, College of Arts and Sciences. University of Kentucky, Lexington, Kentucky, 1964. A replication of the Jonassen study data such as these can add another dimension to content analysis projects.

THESES AND DISSERTATIONS

University of Iowa theses and dissertations are available from the University of Iowa library, Iowa City, Iowa.

277/ Allen, James L.: "Treatment of Labor in the Editorials of Four Chicago Newspapers," unpublished masters thesis, University of Iowa, 1950. Uses sentences as the unit of analysis. Purposes: proportion of favorable, unfavorable, and neutral; frequency of themes; attention to labor; differences in treatment by the four papers over four months.

278/ Arnold, Elizabeth: "A Study of the Editorial Policy of *Better Homes and Gardens,*" unpublished masters thesis, University of Iowa, 1955. Studies approximately one-third of the articles from twelve successive issues. The study attempts to determine if content adhered to the expressed policy of the magazine's editors. Editors' opinions were determined by questionnaire.

279/ Atwood, L. Erwin: "Effects of Congruity and Incongruity on Perceived Source Credibility, Message Acceptance, and Communicator Encoding Performance," unpublished doctoral dissertation, University of Iowa, 1965. Uses three college reporting classes to explore the effects of various combinations of message and source credibility. Uses pre- and post-exposure semantic differential; also analyzes the newspaper stories that class members wrote to determine effect on attribution, direct quotation, and writing time.

280/ Baker, Falcon L.: "The Post-War Rise of How-to-do-it and Self-Help Themes in American Magazines," unpublished masters thesis, University of Iowa, 1954. Designed sample around typical periods. Coordinated with questionnaire to editors.

281/ Bomberger, Russell: "An Analytical Comparison of Scope-Depth Balance with Popularity of General Circulation Weekly Magazines in the United States, 1947–1960," unpublished doctoral dissertation, University of Iowa, 1962. Develops a means of predicting popularity of magazines by determining scope-depth (number-length) ratio of content. It is based on a theory of Dr. Zipf and involves concepts of correlation and regression.

282/ Bowers, David F.: "Changes in Non-Advertising Content of Five Upstate New York Newspapers Subscribing to a Teletypsetter Circuit Operation," unpublished doctoral dissertation, University of Iowa, 1954. Compares newspapers before and after their introduction to TTS to determine any changes or trends in their content. Purposive sampling allows equal representation of all newspapers in the groups (TTS users or chains) and to all days of the week.

283/ Bremner, John B.: "An Analysis of the Content of Catholic Diocesan Newspapers in the United States," unpublished doctoral dissertation, University of Iowa, 1965. Employs content analysis for a study of 40 of 118 American Catholic diocesan weekly newspapers. Tests a number of hypotheses including effects on newspapers of being members of a chain, of circulation, and of size (in number of pages). Reports factors found did not correlate with variables studied.

284/ Brown, Lee M.: "A Content Analysis of Anti-Catholic Documents

Circulated through the Mails during the 1960 Presidential Election Campaign," unpublished masters thesis, University of Iowa, 1961. Thematic analysis (assertions). Excellent example of explanation of procedures and reasons, materials, and findings. Trend charts.

285/ Budd, Richard W.: "A Study of News Concerning the United States in Four Australian and Four New Zealand Metropolitan Daily Newspapers," unpublished masters thesis, University of Iowa, 1962. Includes seventeen subject-matter categories (defined) and three directional categories (defined). Study employs purposive sampling of titles and random (stratified) sample of issues. Devises attention score and a measure of intensity.

286/ Cheng, Pei-wei: "A Study of Four Selected Chinese-Language Newspapers in America," unpublished masters thesis, University of Iowa, 1950. Follows Lasswell's methods to determine if the four papers followed Chinese propaganda themes, of either the Communists or Nationalists. Also counts space and general categories of subjects of stories.

287/ Clark, Jeff: "A Study of the Use of Wire Service Copy by Iowa Evening Newspapers which Receive Wire Service Copy Only from the Iowa-Nebraska Circuit of the Associated Press," unpublished doctoral dissertation, University of Iowa, 1960. The sampling procedure is five days in each of two cycles. Covers a twelve-week period. Stories are classified by central theme, location in the newspapers, and transmission periods. Statistical tests used are chi-square, analysis-of-variance, binomial-probabilities, *t*.

288/ Donohew, Robert Lewis: "Publisher Attitude and Community Conditions as Factors in Newspaper Coverage of a Social Welfare Issue," unpublished doctoral dissertation, University of Iowa, 1965. Through use of a canonical correlation procedure, the author examines the relationship of newspaper coverage of the medical-care-for-the-aged issue to publisher attitude, perceived community opinion, and community conditions that might be related to the issue (such as proportion of the population over age sixty-five). Measures of content direction and display are used in measuring news coverage by a population of newspapers.

289/ Ecker, Judith Koch: "A Content Analysis of Selected Radio and Television Newscasts," unpublished masters thesis, University of Iowa, 1957. A manifest content analysis of radio and TV newscasts gathered from two local radio stations, two local TV stations, and the NBC radio and TV network over a period of one month. It attempts to classify visual presentations and utilizes categories of subject matter, time, and geographic location.

290/ Filer, J. A.: "A New Method–the Quantic–for Content Analysis," unpublished masters thesis, University of Utah, 1958. Use of this technique is demonstrated through analysis of news in the 1952 presidential election.

291/ Griggs, Harry H.: "Coverage of National Economic Conditions by Five Mass Circulation Daily Newspapers during Three Crucial Months of the 1957–1958 Recession," unpublished doctoral dissertation, University of Iowa, 1962. The author gives a clear explanation of his rationale for choosing specific newspapers, months to study, categories, and direction categories. There is a section on validity and reliability and an excellent bibliography.

292/ Haley, Jay Douglas: "Content Analysis of a Film: David and Bathsheba," unpublished masters thesis, Stanford University, Stanford, Calif., 1954. A work that explores the relationship between film content and the audience by employing psychological criteria to the film-audience relationship. Treats meaning on three levels–obvious, social, and unconscious (i.e., mother figure).

293/ Hartmann, Dietrich: "A Comparative Content Analysis of Selected German and American Daily Newspapers," unpublished masters thesis, University of Iowa, 1959. Attempts to select three matched pairs of newspapers. Quantitative findings are used as the basis for inferences about how good a job each newspaper had done in covering selected issues.

294/ Hoar, Frederick M.: "A Content Study of Twenty Midwestern Daily Newspapers ... with Special Attention to the Robert Bednasek Murder Trial," unpublished masters thesis, University of Iowa, 1951. Census of all dailies with a circulation of 100,000 or more published within a radius of 300 miles of Iowa City, plus two Iowa City and one Cedar Rapids dailies. Four levels of analysis are used. The study is worth reading for a general knowledge of content analysis.

295/ Julian, James L.: "An Analysis of Certain Types of Publicity Published in Selected California Daily Newspapers during a Two-Month Period," unpublished doctoral dissertation, University of Iowa, 1956. Rationale for methods is explained. Sampling method for selecting issues is detailed.

296/ Karius, Joseph G.: "Study of the Content of the Milwaukee Daily Newspapers Before and After Their Consolidation of Ownership," unpublished masters thesis, University of Iowa, 1965. Uses constructed-month sample of issues of the *Milwaukee Sentinel* and the *Milwaukee Journal* before and after consolidation. It also uses a mutually exclusive coding system for categories–newspaper sections, comics, sports, editorial, radio-TV—and classification. Employs Budd's attention score. Objective results noted where unanticipated.

297/ McCaffery, Robert J.: "A Study of Personal Columns and Editorials in Iowa Weekly Newspapers," unpublished masters thesis, University of Iowa, 1950. Uses a stratified random sample of newspapers and measurement by column inches. The content is classified into eleven categories, which are clearly defined by examples of content placed in each.

298/ McNamara, Katherine E.: "A Comparative Study of the Reading Ease of Selected Newspapers, House Organs and Business Magazines Published in Iowa," unpublished masters thesis, University of Iowa, 1949. Uses Flesch formula on samples of content from publications chosen. Flesch formula is described.

299/ Merrill, John: "The Image of the U.S. Presented by 10 Mexican Daily Newspapers," unpublished doctoral dissertation, University of Iowa, 1962. Uses three units of analysis—item, space, theme. Thematic analysis is restricted to a few subject areas. Material is classified by subject matter, source of authority, origin, and form (news, opinion, pictorial). It gives a clear definition of subject-matter categories and a description of the coding and recording of data. A questionnaire was used in conjunction with the analysis.

300/ Regier, Hilda M.: "A Content Analysis of *Time* Coverage of the 1960 Presidential Campaign," unpublished masters thesis, University of Iowa, 1965. Attempts to test hypotheses about *Time's* bias for Nixon and against Kennedy in the 1960 presidential election by classification of items as to form, size, and then direction. Coder reliability is a problem: "When the reliability scores for this content analysis are considered, serious doubt arises as to whether any real differences exist between categories adjacent in rank."

301/ Sahu, Biswanath: "A Comparative Study of the News and Views Concerning India in the *New York Times* and the News and Views Concerning the United States Published in the *Times of India*," unpublished masters thesis, University of Iowa, 1965. Employs a rotating sample for selecting issues of the two newspapers to be studied over an eight-month period (first month, first week; second month, second week; and so on). Employs a modification of Budd's attention score in addition to space measurement. The attention score involved size of headline, number of lines in the headline, size of headline type, among other measures including taglines and any accompanying pictures.

302/ Singel, Carmelita G.: "A Study of Some Aspects of the Rise and Development of *Mademoiselle* as Reflected against the Pattern of Fashion Magazines Established by *Vogue*," unpublished masters thesis, University of Iowa, 1957. Qualitative section describes *Mademoiselle* during its early years "in order to give a more realistic picture of the magazine during its period of experimentation and growth." Quantitative analysis is then performed for selected months of four arbitrarily chosen years.

303/ Stone, Vernon A.: "A Content Analysis of the Three Radio Wire Services," unpublished masters thesis, University of Iowa, 1953. Space-time analysis of wires during nine-day period. Categories: subject matter, point of origin, non-news content.

304/ Tabak, Joseph: "A Content Analysis of *United States News and World Report* Magazine during the 1960 Presidential Election Campaign," unpublished masters thesis, University of Iowa, 1961. Employs four direction categories (favorable, unfavorable, neutral, balanced), each well defined and often directed at specific situations.

305/ Talbert, Samuel S.: "The Newspaper in the One-Daily City as a Carrier of Community Opinion," unpublished doctoral dissertation, University of Iowa, 1952. It combines content analysis with mail questionnaire. Content analysis is used to determine the nature and volume of editorial-page content. It is helpful as a guide in classifying editorials.

306/ Turner, William B.: "A Study of Pictorial Treatment in Iowa's Industrial Publications," unpublished masters thesis, University of Iowa, 1953. Combines mail questionnaire to editors with content analysis of their publications. Format and number of pages, amount of space given pictures, and number and content of pictures are studied.

307/ Whitley, Frank V.: "Criticism of Public Education in Lay Magazines," unpublished masters thesis, University of Iowa, 1955. The author selected his period of study by determining when educators' concern over criticism rose sharply. He used a special index to locate articles, and thematic categories of criticisms. The study notes trends in volume of articles and in emphasis on subject matter and includes some impressionistic analysis.

308/ Widmar, Barbara Haardt: "Coverage of Three International Crises of 1960 by Selected Iowa Daily Newspapers," unpublished masters thesis, University of Iowa. 1964. It uses three foreign-affairs issues and studies daily newspaper coverage for a time period before the crises broke. Also studies coverage of each crisis in relationship to index of continuing minor crises in countries where the major events took place.

309/ Yu, Frederick Teh-Chi: "The Treatment of China in Four Chicago Daily Newspapers July 1 through December 31, 1949," unpublished doctoral dissertation, University of Iowa, 1951. For a sample of titles, the author considered wire service or the source for material about China and the editorial point of view with respect to China. He analyzed content by column inches and number of items and used subject-matter classifications. Some thematic analysis of selected content; attention score used as a measure of plan. Good explanation of thematic analysis based on assertions.

index